# CFA VOYSEY

STUART DURANT

**Architectural Monographs No 19**

# CFA VOYSEY
## STUART DURANT

**A.P.** ACADEMY EDITIONS / ST MARTIN'S PRESS

Architectural Monographs No 19
Editorial Offices
42 Leinster Gardens London W2 3AN

ISSN 0141-2191

Editorial and Design Team
Andreas Papadakis (Publisher)
Andrea Bettella (Senior Designer)
Helen Castle, Justin Ageros, Lisa Kosky

Photography
The majority of photographic material is taken from contemporary sources and publications. Colour photographs taken by Robert Oerlemans of Moorcrag and Broadleys were specially commissioned by Academy.

Publisher's note
Work on this monograph started well over a decade ago with the help of John Brandon-Jones who enabled me to start collecting together material with the loan of his scrapbook – an extensive record of Voysey's career including texts and photographs. During this period, research was continued by a number of staff at Academy Editions. The project, however, would not have been possible without Stuart Durant who has not only provided the main essay and project descriptions but has also been instrumental in choosing articles and images.                          *ACP*

*Cover:* View of Moorcrag, Lake Windermere, Cumbria, 1898; *P2:* View of Broadleys from Lake, Lake Windermere, Cumbria, 1898.

First published in Great Britain in 1992 by
ACADEMY EDITIONS
An imprint of the Academy Group Ltd
42 Leinster Gardens London W2 3AN

ISBN 1 85490 031 5 (HB)
ISBN 1 85490 032 3 (PB)

Published in the United States of America by
ST MARTIN'S PRESS
175 Fifth Avenue, New York, NY 10010

ISBN 0-312-05199-9 (HB)
ISBN 0-312-05205-7 (PB)

Printed and bound in Singapore

# CONTENTS

Stuart Durant *CFA Voysey, 1857-1941*                               6

## PROJECTS
Cottage for Mr and Mrs CFA Voysey                                  22
An Artist's Cottage                                                23
14 South Parade                                                    24
Cottage, Bishop's Itchington                                       26
Walnut Tree Farm                                                   27
Studio House                                                       30
The Hans Road Houses                                               31
Perrycroft                                                         34
Lowicks                                                            38
Annesley Lodge                                                     40
Greyfriars                                                         44
New Place                                                          45
Norney                                                             48
Broadleys                                                          50
Moorcrag                                                           62
Spade House                                                        76
The Orchard                                                        78
Vodin                                                              80
The Pastures                                                       82
White Horse Inn                                                    84
Hollymount                                                         85
House in Aswan                                                     86
The Homestead                                                      88
Littleholme, Guildford                                             92
Littleholme, Kendal                                                94
Lodge Style                                                        96

## ESSAYS
An Interview with CFA Voysey, Architect and Designer – *The Studio*   98
The Revival of English Domestic Architecture – *The Studio*        104
Notes on Country and Suburban Houses – *Horace Townsend*           110

## WRITINGS BY CFA VOYSEY
Ideas in Things                                                   112
Individuality                                                     126
On Concrete                                                       134

Chronology                                                        136
Selected Unexecuted Projects                                      138
Selected Surviving Projects                                       140
Bibliography                                                      142

PORTRAIT OF CFA VOYSEY, IN HIS 50s, WEARING A LAPELESS JACKET AND SILK SCARF MADE TO HIS OWN DESIGN

# STUART DURANT

## CFA VOYSEY, 1857-1941

'I make no claim to anything new,' Voysey wrote to the editor of *Architects' Journal* in March 1935, '. . . like many others, I followed some old traditions and avoided some others . . . steel construction and reinforced concrete are the real culprits responsible for the ultra-modern architecture of today.' Despite this seemingly reactionary statement, Voysey's great achievement was to bring about a vital symbiosis between innovation and tradition.

The fact is, Voysey was a Victorian. And he was nurtured in the richest of Victorian environments – the intellectual home.

He might have something to teach us: his architecture is 'green', his buildings are made from simple materials. Now, we could build in the way he did. It might seem expensive; but the sheer pleasure well-made things bring would more than compensate.

Building in a labour-intensive way could be rewarding, too. William Morris once said in a lecture – *Of the Origins of Ornamental Art*, given in 1883 – 'Machines should never be used for doing work in which men can take pleasure'. While we may never arrive at the Morrisian millennium, we need, as automation proceeds, to find worthwhile things for people to do. Building well, for posterity, could be one of them.

His utterances are always at their most profound in his architecture. He did theorise more than most of his architectural contemporaries. What Voysey has to say is worth reading and on occasions it can be psychologically revealing. But he is not, it should be said, the intellectual peer of Lethaby, the leading architect-theoretician of the Arts and Crafts, still less of Morris or Ruskin.

He was the first domestic architect to gain an international reputation. Of course, long before Voysey, there had been Palladio, on a grander scale, but at the turn of the century when Voysey came to the fore, Palladio's reputation – as it always had done – rested with a small, architecturally literate elite. One did not need to be a scholar to appreciate Voysey's work.

Voysey could be described as the first popular architect. Any amateur could look through widely circulated art magazines – like *The Studio*, founded in 1893, or the Munich magazine *Dekorative Kunst*, founded in 1897 – where one could find all one needed to know about Voysey's houses, his furniture or his decoration.

The Voysey House was picturesque, with gentle references to unspecified vernacular traditions. Unlike some of his Arts and Crafts colleagues, Voysey did not resort to a stilted borrowing of arcane traditional details. The Voysey House was convenient, informal, economical to build and maintain. It seemed refreshingly new. There is a Protean *fin-de-siècle* vitality about a Voysey House.

Occasionally, Voysey's work has a quality which prompts one to think of the work of some of the well-known children's illustrators of the 1880s, 1890s such as Walter Crane, Randolph Caldecott, Kate Greenaway and Beatrix Potter. Any comparison between Voysey's work and that of once-fashionable illustrators might be thought to be an unflattering one but there is in his work a certain artificiality – an indefinable quaintness. This is characteristic of much British art and design of the 1880s and 1890s.

It is not the intention here to trivialise Voysey. There is nothing in the least trivial in his work; it has stood the test of time in practical and aesthetic terms. But no great architect before had possessed such delicacy and lightness of touch.

Charles Francis Annesley Voysey was born on May 28th, 1857. Pugin had been dead for almost five years, but Scott, Street and Butterfield who were all great church architects were in their prime. Religion and architecture were the two great Victorian obsessions. Voysey was himself the eldest son of a clergyman, the Reverend Charles Voysey (1828-1912). His mother, Mary Edlin, was the daughter of a banker.

Voysey's childhood was disrupted by an event which it is difficult to fully comprehend some 120 years later. The stark fact is Charles Voysey was dismissed from the Anglican church by being 'deprived of his living' for teaching unapproved doctrine. In the latter part of the 20th century, when a lukewarm doctrinal liberalism prevails, this may not appear to be a very significant matter.

Such was not the case in the 19th century. As a result of the social and psychological upheavals brought about by industrialisation, by the vast, destabilising migrations of ordinary people, and above all by the advance of scientific materialism, religion had become a field for intensive speculation. John Henry Newman's writings, in particular his spiritual autobiography *Apologia pro Vita Sua*, reflect the often high intellectual quality of such speculation.

Every scandal concerning the Church was of profound interest. Of these, the greatest, of course, was Newman's defection to the Church of Rome on October 8, 1845 – a trauma for Oxford and an unmitigated disaster for the Anglican Church. In comparison the heresy of Charles Voysey, the vicar of the obscure parish of Healaugh, near York, may have only been of minor importance but enough to have caused regional concern.

Charles Voysey had simply published controversial sermons, one of which was 'Is every statement in the Bible about our Heavenly Father true?' Nevertheless, the Healaugh affair profoundly influenced the lives of all the Voysey family. Rev Voysey was given the opportunity to retract his ideas, but he chose instead the lonely path of the heretic and the martyr. He was a man with inflexible opinions – a characteristic that he passed on to his son.

Voysey was 12 when the final judgement against his father was delivered in the House of Lords on February 11, 1871. By this time the family had moved to London and Charles Voysey had begun to preach on his own account, soon drawing a sizeable congregation.

He founded the Theistic Church, which was to be situated in a small street off Piccadilly. One may deduce from such a prosperous location that Theism appealed to the educated middle class who seem to have been prepared to invest in what Charles Voysey described as a new religion in its own right. He was sympathetic towards science and Theism could readily accommodate the idea of evolution. Charles Voysey considered Theism itself to be part of an evolutionary process operating within religion; the God of the Theists was not the wrathful God of the Old Testament.

Charles Voysey, a fine preacher, and a prolific publisher of sermons, nevertheless bequeathed no enduring theological legacy. With his death in 1912, Theism evaporated into the ether, though Voysey's brother became a Unitarian minister; Theism was in fact in some ways quite close to Unitarianism.

At first educated at home by his father, Voysey, at 13, was sent to Dulwich College as a day boy. Like many similar schools, it was to undergo a considerable expansion during the Victorian era. The

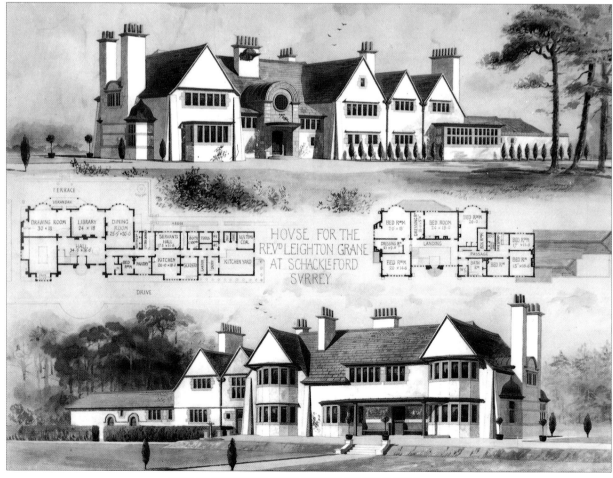

*ABOVE*: CFA VOYSEY IN HIS OFFICE AT YORK PLACE; *BELOW*: NORNEY, 1897

new buildings of the 1860s, in a North Italian early Renaissance style, were by the younger Charles Barry (1823-1900), the son of Sir Charles Barry, the designer – with the aid of Pugin – of the Houses of Parliament. Might these vigorous, if rather brash, buildings have turned the young Voysey's thoughts towards architecture? Surely Soane's sombre Dulwich Picture Gallery, which was not far away, would not have inspired him in the least. Soane's reputation, which had been undermined by Pugin's attack in *Contrasts* of 1836, was still at a low ebb in the 1870s.

The redoubtable JCL Sparkes was art master at Dulwich. He had a remarkable gift for recognising ability in the young. Two important late Victorian painters, Stanhope Forbes, (1857-1947) and Henry La Thangue (1859-1929) were both at Dulwich with Voysey and were taught by Sparkes. (In the early 1900s Voysey designed a house in Bedford Park for a La Thangue which was never built.) One may surmise that because he had only a modest gift for drawing from the human figure, that were most likely plaster casts of approved classical figures, Voysey's talents as an artist did not impress Sparkes.

Voysey did not thrive academically at Dulwich though he was able enough intellectually. He may have suffered from what is now described as 'learning difficulties'. Apparently he was an erratic speller. Perhaps family tensions, induced by the scandal of Healaugh, may have been damaging to a boy on the verge of adolescence.

After 18 months at Dulwich, Voysey was withdrawn and educated at home until the eve of his 17th birthday. It could have been that architecture was selected for him as a career while he was at Dulwich. Sparkes could have suggested the idea – a straw of comfort to a father despairing of his son's prospects. However, his paternal grandfather Annesley Voysey, 1794-1834, had been a successful architect. This is the most likely reason for Voysey's entry into architecture – a profession which did not have the status it was to acquire in the present century.

Voysey was articled to John Pollard Seddon (1827-1906) on 11 May, 1874. Here begins the better documented part of his life, although it should be pointed out that, as with so many architects, there is all too often a dearth of hard biographical information. Seddon was at the height of his powers. He was a sound Gothic Revivalist with a good, primarily ecclesiastical, practice. Seddon's architecture was restrained and practical, but he lacked, perhaps, the brilliance of Butterfield or Street, or still more, William Burges. Seddon, nevertheless, was an ideal mentor. Voysey learned restraint and rationality during his five years with Seddon.

After leaving Seddon, Voysey assisted Henry Saxon Snell (1830-1904) for a short time. Snell successfully specialised in the design of hospitals and charitable institutions he was the author of *Charitable and Parochial Buildings*, 1881, and, with Dr FJ Mouat, of *Hospital Construction and Management*, 1883. Among his London buildings were: Emmanuel School, Wandsworth, part of the recently demolished hospital in Fulham Palace Road, and the hospital in Archway Road.

Although Voysey did not relish the work in the Snell office, which he found dull, he evidently acquired enough specialised technical knowledge there to design a sanatorium for Teignmouth between 1882 and 1884. Although this ultimately came to nothing, it seems to have been his first major project. It is worth pointing out that in 1899 Voysey was to design a cottage hospital at Halwill, near Beaworthy, Devon, which is still standing. He probably learned little concerning the art of architecture during his time in the Snell office, although it would have reinforced his belief that buildings should be, above all, practical, and it fostered an interest in ventilation which continued throughout his career.

Of supreme importance in Voysey's development was the period he spent with George Devey (1820-1886), the country house architect. Devey was a member of Charles Voysey's Theistic Church and a generous subscriber to its funds, and Voysey would

have met him through this connection. He worked for Devey for nearly two years as an 'improver', that is a young architect who, having completed his articles, sought to gain professional experience. Generally, improvers were not paid.

Without question, Devey was an architect of the first rank. Less of a extrovert than Richard Norman Shaw, he has, until comparatively recently, been treated as a somewhat shadowy, even minor, figure. He may yet be the last major Victorian architect to be rediscovered. (Jill Allibone's recent study reveals his stature and Mark Girouard in *The Victorian Country House*, first published in 1971, also acknowledged his qualities.)

Devey's clients were mainly members of the landed gentry and, not surprisingly, Devey took a keen interest in vernacular building. He would, of course, have seen much of it during his visits to country estates. The RIBA possesses several volumes of his sketches of cottages in their settings. An abortive scheme, for a middle-class housing development in Northampton of around 1876 shows that Devey was capable of devising delightful and varied houses – as Shaw had done at Bedford Park at about the same time. Two of Devey's smaller house types for Northampton resemble the kind of houses which Parker and Unwin were to design for Letchworth Garden City 25 years later. Some of Devey's projected Northampton houses suggest a vernacular influence.

Voysey is said to have designed some cottages for Devey in Northamptonshire, where he had some land though it has not been possible to trace these. One can safely assume that they would have had the Devey imprint. There is a distinctly Devey-like quality in several of Voysey's earliest schemes that is most apparent in the work that he did before he attained full autonomy as an architect.

Voysey, then, had three able teachers – Seddon, Snell and Devey – before he started practice on his own. Like so many of his contemporaries, he had also come under the influence, through their writings, of two towering figures: Ruskin and Pugin. Throughout his life, his writings and his attitudes were to reveal his commitment to their ideals. Voysey cannot be called the last Ruskinian as there are too many candidates for that honour but he could well be called the last Puginian.

And what of Morris? Voysey certainly admired Morris' decorative designs. After all, what designer maturing in the 1880s did not? But he abhorred Morris' Socialism, which he equated with what he called collectivism. Voysey stood for 'individuality'. He proclaimed his faith in it in his short book *Individuality* written in 1915, when, under the influence of universal war madness, individuality was trampled upon.

Voysey set up his own practice in late 1881, or early 1882, in Queen Anne's Gate. He moved very shortly. He declared on his curious, one supposes jesting, change-of-address card:

Unto alle and sondrie. Know ye hereby yt ye Architect Master CFA Voysey heretofore of Queen Anne's Gate hath now removed unto ye more commodious premises situate at ye Broadway Chambers, Westminster. Here from henceforth all ye craft of ye master architect will be exercised.

Very early in his career, Voysey entered a competition for the Admiralty offices in Whitehall, but the design was unplaced. No record seems to exist of it – it would have been instructive to see how he would have handled a monumental design at this stage. Monumentality was never his forte.

However, a very early design by Voysey does survive in published form. This was for the sanatorium at Teignmouth in Devon (1882-84). It is only known through a reproduction of a drawing in 'CFA Voysey', *Dekorative Kunst 1*; Voysey's first major appearance in a Continental periodical. This was a copiously illustrated and extensive article which could possibly have been by Hermann Muthesius who was later to publish *Das Englische Haus* and was in London at this time. Voysey was obviously responsible for the selection of illustrations in the article. He, at least,

*ABOVE*: WALNUT TREE FARM, 1890; *BELOW*: THE PASTURES, 1901

considered the sanatorium project important.

All that is shown of the sanatorium, built for the Teignmouth Sanatorium Company, is what is probably an elevation facing towards the sea. It is quite evidently an institutional building, but one that is made more congenial by the addition of a certain amount of picturesque and medievalising detail. Voysey also makes use of the diaper-patterned brickwork favoured by Devey, which he was to use in another early project – the house with an octagonal hall. There is a certain clumsiness in the sanatorium design, which is not altogether unpleasing, but the elevation is confident. It does not immediately strike one as the work of a very young man.

Of course, Voysey, like all young architects, did not find commissions easy to come by. A friend – AH Mackmurdo (1852-1942) – the pivotal member of The Century Guild – a Morrisian co-operative of designers which sought 'to render all branches of art the sphere no longer of the tradesman but the artist' – encouraged Voysey to take up designing textiles and wallpapers in order to supplement his small income from architecture and he was to become extremely successful at this. His status as a decorative designer equals that of Walter Crane, or Lewis F Day.

Since the Modern Movement, which anathematised decoration, it has often been assumed that the spatial and organisational skills of the architect are very different from those of the designer of decoration. This is not the case. It is very easy, in fact, to cite architects who have excelled at decorative design: Robert Adam, Pugin, Butterfield, Burges, Philip Webb, Viollet-le-Duc, Otto Wagner, Frank Furness, Sullivan, Guimard, Van de Velde, Mackintosh and Hoffmann for example. MH Baillie Scott (1865-1945), in many ways Voysey's principal rival as a designer of small-scale country houses, was also an accomplished designer of decoration. The ability to generate pattern is closely allied to the ability to manipulate geometric forms so essential to architects.

Among Voysey's early and unexecuted projects is a design for his own cottage. This is probably the most important among the early projects in tracing the evolution of the Voysey House. The half-timbered cottage probably dates from 1885, the year in which he married Mary Maria Evans. It was illustrated for the first time in *The British Architect XXX*, 1888. The cottage was also illustrated in the October 1894 issue of *The Studio. The Studio* was to illustrate much of Voysey's early work and such publicity must have brought him clients. The almost excessive half-timbering was 'solid and tarred' – Voysey's drawing seems to emphasise this – and filled in with 'breeze concrete'. One would have expected a more traditional material – if he had been an obsessive medievalist.

The cottage was roofed with green slate and its external woodwork was a bright, cheerful, green which, it was said, would harmonise with the surrounding countryside. (Interestingly enough, Christopher Dresser (1834-1904) a prominent commercial designer who had strong ideas on colour, commented on just how much he disliked seeing natural and artificial greens in juxtaposition.) The cottage was buttressed at ground floor level in order to reduce costs by lessening the thicknesses of the walls.

The plan of the cottage is somewhat unusual as the largest room is described as a 'living and work room'. It is the only resemblance that the cottage actually bears to a country labourer's dwelling. Here is the space, dominating the whole house where Voysey intended to work. The cottage has something of the air of a bachelor's residence, certainly its plan does not suggest the home of a *paterfamilias*. Leading off the living and work room is a narrow picture-gallery where Voysey intended to display his own work. This is the first example of the Voysey House. It is also the earliest of his architectural drawings of Voysey's to have survived.

Another early design was for a medium-sized house which was first illustrated in *The British Architect, XXXI*, 1889. It is possible that this actually antedates the cottage. This house, which has an octagonal hall, resembles one of the larger house types which

Devey had designed for the abortive housing scheme in Northampton. One may also detect the influence of Richard Norman Shaw.

With its half-timbering, its prominent belvedere, its dressed stone contrasted with patterned brickwork, and its unmistakably Victorian bay window, the house can properly be described as picturesquely eclectic. The circulation of the house depends upon the octagonal hall from which all the principal rooms open; above it is a gallery linking the main upstairs rooms. The plan, despite a degree of ingenuity, is not entirely convincing for Voysey, though a perfectly reasonable creator of plans, was not a virtuoso planner like Shaw or Baillie Scott.

Although the house with the octagonal hall, unlike the cottage, is not instantly recognisable as a Voysey House, there is a refinement in its proportions that does suggest his hand. Voysey made use of unusual proportions and generally favoured an exaggerated horizontality which contrasts with Pugin's over-stressed verticality. There would appear, however, to be no formal mathematical basis to his system of proportions – if system one designates it. Like Ruskin, Voysey despised those things which he considered mathematically commensurable and hence crudely mechanistic. Voysey's proportions, like many aspects of his design, depend upon a sound empiricism tempered by a highly individual sensibility.

The design for the house with the octagonal hall does not seem to have brought Voysey any clients – possibly because it suggested that he had rather fanciful ideas. Besides, who would trust a young and unknown architect with such an apparently costly project? However, the drawings of his own more modest cottage which had appeared in *The British Architect* did bring him a client. In 1888, the same year in which the cottage drawings were published, Voysey was commissioned to design a small house for M H Lakin at Bishop's Itchington, in Warwickshire. This was to be a modified version of the cottage. The half-timbering was omitted – very likely to reduce costs – and the entire wall-surfaces of the house were covered with rough-cast. This was the first Voysey House to have been built. It was called 'The Cottage' which is a name that Voysey seems to have suggested himself on later occasions.

Although it is all too easy to recognise that The Cottage had antecedents in the smaller domestic work of Gothic Revivalists – Seddon, of course, or Butterfield, Philip Webb, or Devey, with his paraphrases of vernacular buildings – the Bishop's Itchington house has much that is positively new about it. Voysey succeeded here in blending vernacular, medieval, and purely innovative elements in a refreshingly unselfconscious way.

Voysey recognised that a scholarly, not to say pedantic, borrowing from the past would lead only to an architecture which was remote from contemporary reality. 'Revivalism must involve the sacrifice of fitness,' he was to say in 'Ideas in Things' – two articles in *The Arts Connected with Building*, a collection of essays by a number of arts and crafts designers, edited by T Raffles Davison and published in 1909.

In the same year as the design for Lakin, 1888, Voysey produced a preliminary design for a house for Mrs Forster in South Parade, Bedford Park, Chiswick. The earliest garden suburb, Bedford Park had been founded in 1875 and was effectively the test-bed for the garden city, in terms of house types at least. Norman Shaw was its principal architect though protégés of his were also involved. The projected Forster House differs quite markedly from the neighbouring Shaw Houses which, although representing a new approach to middle-class housing, make reference to the Early Renaissance in English architecture. They are frequently rich in moulded brick detail, inspired by nearby red-brick Kew Palace which was originally built as a London merchant's house in 1631.

The Forster house is plainer than the Shaw Houses, only on the ground floor is the brickwork revealed. The porch has a low Tudor, or late-medieval, arch surrounded with moulded bricks. The wide and stoutly constructed front door has the wrought-iron hinges of

NORNEY, 1897

which Voysey was so fond. The deep eaves are supported by slender wrought-iron brackets. The bay windows, with leaded glazing on the ground and first floor, are reminiscent of those to be found in speculative suburban houses of the 1920s and 1930s. In many ways, the projected Forster house would fit comfortably into almost any prosperous pre-war London suburbs. Had it been widely publicised, one might have been able to suggest that it was the very prototype of the London suburban house. Voysey's proportions, however, give the house a look of solidity combined with elegance and such qualities were not often seen in suburban architecture.

In 1889 *The British Architect, XXXI*, illustrated a 'tower house' by Voysey. It would not have been cheap to build. Possibly Voysey simply used the design to publicise his ideas. The 'tower house' had four floors and, like the unbuilt cottage for himself of 1885, it was capped with heavy half-timbering. It was conspicuously buttressed to the second floor and clad with rough-cast. It has an assertiveness which only the most accomplished architectural personalities can achieve without descending to vulgarity. In 1903, Voysey was to revive the 'tower house' idea in an unrealised project at Bognor, Sussex, for W Ward Higgs. This was a five-floor house without buttresses, and a band of windows on the top floor to enable the owner to enjoy the panorama.

The Forster House, Bedford Park, as it was finally to be built in 1891, was to represent a compromise between the first project and the 'tower house'. Like the first design, it was conspicuously different from the adjoining Shaw houses. It was plain, entirely covered with rough-cast, with stone mullions and leaded lights. There were still the wide eaves and the wrought-iron brackets. In the 1890s Bedford Park was still fashionable among artists, or at least the artistically inclined and the Forster house – easily seen from the District Line – would have served as an excellent London showcase for Voysey. Almost every Londoner interested in developments in the arts would have seen it. The Forster House effectively launched Voysey's career.

Another early Voysey House was Walnut Tree Farm, Castlemorton, near Malvern, which was designed for RH Cazalet in 1890. This also appeared in *The British Architect, XXXIV*, 1890. Because of its comparatively remote location, Walnut Tree Farm made a lesser impact than the Bedford Park house. It has a number of features which were to be found in the 1885 cottage, including buttressing at ground floor level, deep eaves and a rough-cast finish. The house has four dormer windows, one of which is distinctly larger than the others, varied window sizes, a corner bay which is five sides of an octagon to trap the sun, and prominent chimneys, the sides of which slope dramatically. These serve to give this comparatively small building an air of complexity, or even fussiness.

W Alexander Harvey, the architect of the Cadbury family's ideal industrial town of Bourneville, designed a private house for JH Barlow which suggests the inspiration of Walnut Tree Farm. This is illustrated in H Whitehouse: 'Bourneville. A study in housing reform', *The Studio, XXIV*, 1903. A number of Bourneville designs by Harvey have Voysey-like features including buttresses. While it is common knowledge that Voysey had a very considerable influence in his day, it is not easy to cite such textbook disciples.

In 1891-92, Voysey was commissioned by Archibald Grove to design a pair of houses for Hans Road in Knightsbridge. The fact that he was asked to design houses for what was obviously an expensive site indicates that, though still in his 30s, Voysey's practice was beginning to flourish. Originally there were to have been three houses – one for Grove himself and the others for letting. But Voysey's friend AH Mackmurdo was subsequently commissioned to design the third house. This is said by John Brandon-Jones to have led to a rift in a once warm friendship. Reasonably close at hand are to be found a number of imaginative town houses by such major contemporary architects as Shaw, EW Godwin and JJ Stevenson – nearly all are in a style that can be loosely described as

Queen Anne. These houses were located conveniently close to the South Kensington Museum – later to be re-named The Victoria and Albert Museum – and for two decades the area had been associated with a well-healed aestheticism.

Voysey's Hans Road Houses reflect, to a degree, the influence of Shaw, though they are simpler. Stone mullions give them a somewhat medieval appearance; rooms are panelled and a grand room at the rear of each house is achieved by the introduction of a mezzanine floor – a device that Voysey undoubtedly borrowed from Shaw, whose complex multi-level sections were marvels of ingenuity. Shaw's sections and plans seem to echo the complex mechanisms of late 19th-century society. How complex these seem when compared with the sections of 18th-century town houses.

The contrast between Mackmurdo's Hans Road House and Voysey's pair is extreme: Voysey appears assured but inclined towards idiosyncrasy, though not eccentricity. Mackmurdo, on the other hand, teeters towards an unscholarly classicism. (This can be confirmed by studying his curious house at 25 Cadogan Gardens, not far from Sloane Square.) The writer, Julian Russell Sturgis, for whom, in 1896, Voysey was to design one of his finest houses – Greyfriars, on the Hog's Back, near Guildford – lived in one of the Hans Road Houses. This is how he would have come to know Voysey's work and thus come to admire his practical sensibility.

Perrycroft, the first of Voysey's eight or so larger houses, was designed for JW Wilson, MP, between 1893 and 1894. The site chosen was a fine one: at Colwall, near Malvern, which has views over the Malvern hills. The house cost a little under 5000 pounds, or approximately one million pounds of today's money, excluding the cost of the site. Perrycroft has the roughcast and buttresses of Voysey's earlier houses and the ceilings were similarly low. There is a small tower, obviously intended primarily for effect; but monumentality and display are otherwise eschewed in true Arts and Crafts style. Perrycroft was widely publicised, being illustrated in *The British Architect, XLII*, 1894, as well as in the important article in *Dekorative Kunst* of 1897.

Perrycroft was followed, in 1894, by Lowicks at Frensham, in Surrey, for EJ Horniman, of the well-known tea importing family. The Hornimans were interested in avant-garde architecture. FJ Horniman, MP, commissioned CH Townsend in 1900 to design the Horniman Museum, Forest Hill. (*The Studio* called this 'frank and fearless'.) Lowicks, which was more modest in size than Perrycroft, heralds the houses of Voysey's mature period. Although a timbered dormer reminds one of Walnut Tree Farm, it is far plainer – and plainer even than Perrycroft.

Then came a large project, unfortunately to be an abortive one, on which Voysey worked in 1894-95. This was for a house for the Earl of Lovelace, which was to be built on a site in the garden of Ockham Park – a house built by Hawksmoor in 1725, near the village of Ockham, in the countryside near Ripley in Surrey. The very existence of such an ambitious project indicates that Voysey had learned how to deal with aristocratic clients during the time he had spent with George Devey. The house was low; buttressed and with the typical slate roof, but it was much larger than any of Voysey's built houses. The Ockham Park house has the same sort of awkward quality which Norney Grange of 1897, another big Surrey house, was to have. Voysey was not at his best with large, grandiloquent houses. He did, in fact, build a modest cottage – Pevsner calls it 'primitive' – for one of the Earl's Ockham estate workers. He also built a group of thatched cottages, at Elmesthorpe, Hinckley, Leicestershire, between 1895 and 1896, for the Earl.

In 1895, Voysey designed a house for his father. George Devey, on his death in 1886, had left Charles Voysey a personal legacy of some 2000 pounds which was a considerable sum at the time. It is very possible that this money went towards the house. The house was called Annesley Lodge, after Charles Voysey's architect father. Situated in Hampstead, it was illustrated in both *The British*

*ABOVE*: THE HOMESTEAD, 1905; *BELOW*: LOWICKS, 1894

*Architect* and *The Studio*. The house is L-shaped and represents the Voysey House in its final and complete form.

Greyfriars, one of Voysey's finest houses, was designed in 1896 and if he had designed nothing else Voysey's reputation would still have been one to reckon with. The house was originally known as Merlshanger, then as Wancote. It is situated on the Hog's Back, not far from Guildford. The client, an interesting one, was Julian Russell Sturgis, 1848-1904, a widely travelled and successful novelist. Sturgis also wrote verse, including the lyrics for Sir Arthur Sullivan's *Ivanhoe* and Sir Charles Villiers Stanford's version of *Much Ado about Nothing*. Voysey's perspective of the house shows Sturgis standing in front of it with his head in a book. The house is narrow, so that as many rooms as possible can face the view, which is among the finest in the Home Counties. ('Hang the cost man,' said Bossinney, the young architect, in Galsworthy's *Forsyte Saga*, 'look at the view.') The house, as well as being narrow, is also low but it is not in the least self-effacing. It could, in fact, be described as the boldest of all Voysey's houses.

Although it is impossible to measure with the precise historical significance of Greyfriars, it is reasonable to claim, that after Philip Webb's Red House for William Morris of 1859, it was the most remarkable British house of the 19th century. Its principal impact, however, was made in the early 20th century. Indeed, at first glance, the house seems to hint at the coming century. In actuality, Greyfriars can be set readily within the Gothic canon or more precisely the Puginian canon.

Greyfriars was the most widely illustrated of all Voysey's houses. It was to appear in innumerable British and European publications. The most important of these was Hermann Muthesius' enormously influential *Das Englische Haus*, Berlin, 1904-05. In the 1890s, this conception could only have come from Voysey. Unfortunately, Greyfriars was altered in 1913 and the startling clarity of its conception, like an elegant equation, has been all but obscured. The situation is worsened by the addition of unsympathetic outbuildings. It is conceivable, however, that Greyfriars could be reinstated without great difficulty, as one of the most original buildings of the 19th century.

In 1897, Voysey designed another Surrey house – Norney Grange, near Eashing, West of Godalming. This was for the Reverend W Leighton Crane who, like many Victorian clergymen, must have been moneyed. Norney, which is quite large, is an awkward building. Ian Nairn and Pevsner writing in *The Buildings of England* are not kind about Norney:

> Voysey is here almost making clichés out of his own style, particularly in the entrance front with the ugly doorway and the asymmetrically battered gabled wings. The house also has Voysey's disconcerting quality of appearing more solid the longer the viewer looks at it.

The front elevation of Norney has an odd feel to it. It seems almost as if Voysey was trying to make points. One is reminded, a little, of the excessively didactic quality of some of Philip Webb's houses – Clouds, or Standen, for example. The garden elevation, which is unaffected and simple, is entirely successful.

In the same year in which he designed Norney, Voysey was to design New Place, a house at Haslemere, Surrey, for the publisher AM Stedman, later Sir Algernon Methuen. Voysey was now 40 and his reputation was growing. With its general air of complexity, New Place does not possess the serene resolution of Greyfriars. Nevertheless, it demonstrated that Voysey could orchestrate a range of architectural elements – bays of different types, chimneys, gables, dormers – with great skill. All things considered, New Place is among Voysey's better houses; certainly, it does not exhibit the infelicities of Norney.

Broadleys, overlooking Lake Windermere, was designed in 1898, for A Currer Briggs, the son of a Yorkshire colliery owner. Later in 1904-05, Voysey was to design housing and a miners' institute for the employees of Briggs and Son. This implies that Currer Briggs had progressive social ideas for his time. Broadleys, with Greyfriars, is deservedly the best known of Voysey's houses. Like Greyfriars, Muthesius was to make much of it.

Broadleys was intended for the summer months, but it as a sober house it has none of the frivolity often associated with late-Victorian holiday homes. Like Greyfriars, the principal elevation is the one which faces towards the finest view. In both cases this is not the domain of the householder. In the 18th century the builder of the fine house possessed the view himself. This serves to remind us of two things. Firstly, Voysey's clients were, for the most part, bourgeois intellectuals with a taste for the arts – a new class of consumers which had multiplied since the 1850s. Secondly, Ruskin had popularised the idea that the contemplation of landscape, as the handiwork of God – however defined – was morally uplifting. This thinking, conveyed in such writings as *Modern Painters*, quickly passed into the national unconscious. Ruskin himself had a house in the Lake District, built on a site not very different from Broadleys, at Brantwood, on Coniston Water, which he had bought – unseen – in September 1871, after merely hearing its description.

Broadleys can best be seen from a boat in the lake. On the lake elevation, it has three stone-mullioned bays, almost like the bow windows of Regency houses. The central bay, like the bay in Greyfriars, is used to light a double height hall. The partial symmetry of the house is disrupted by a massive chimney and a small, round, porthole-like window placed to the right of the central bay. The composition of the lake elevation is of great subtlety. How easy it would have been for Voysey to have reduced it to total symmetry. Broadleys appears in the film based on John Fowles' book *The French Lieutenant's Woman* where it was used to affirm the spiritual escape of the heroine – played by Meryl Streep – from the fetters of a stifling Victorian morality. Although Fowles' book is set rather earlier than the time when Broadleys was built, the anachronism can be condoned for Broadleys, like Greyfriars, does seem to stand for a kind of enlightenment.

Nairn and Pevsner remarked in their guide to the buildings of Surrey that Voysey had 'much greater artistic integrity than Lutyens, but less talent . . . Voysey houses are the same everywhere – this can be a serious failing – and his style did not alter much throughout his life.' These remarks can certainly not be dismissed lightly. Integrity? Well, Lutyens, desperate for worldly success, always seized the main chance. Less talent? That is a difficult question to address.

The fact is, Voysey invented a style, whereas Lutyens – with virtuosity and, on occasions, bravura – adapted styles; initially, the vernacular South of England style and latterly, the English Palladian style. That some of Lutyens' houses are of a very high aesthetic quality is impossible to deny – but, using Greyfriars and Broadleys, Voysey's two finest houses, as examplars, it is reasonable to claim that Voysey was indeed a greater innovator than Lutyens.

Were Voysey's houses the same wherever they were built? There is a degree of truth in the assertion that they were, although all Voysey's lakeland houses – after Broadleys came Moorcrag, Windermere, 1898-99, and Littleholme, Kendal, 1909 – have an appropriate northern sternness. So, too, did an unexecuted house, the stone construction untypically left exposed – at Glassonby, Kirkoswald, Cumberland, of 1898.

And the final point to be considered in these diversionary paragraphs – did Voysey's style remain static? No, not exactly, But, after a remarkable and swift evolution – an evolution towards a particular kind of perfection – beginning with the Teignmouth sanatorium project of the early 1880s and culminating in Broadleys of 1898 – Voysey's powers do seem to have begun to diminish. This is also reflected in his decorative design.

One can only speculate on the reasons for his decline. John Brandon-Jones has hinted that Voysey suffered from a gastric

*ABOVE AND BELOW*: OFFICES, NEW BROAD STREET, LONDON, 1909

ulcer. This, in the early years of the century, would have been less susceptible to treatment than it is today. Pain, rather than arrogance, may have made Voysey a difficult man with whom to work. A reputation as such would surely not have endeared him to the kind of client he needed to cultivate in order to display his abilities to the full. This is not to dismiss Voysey's later work, but, undeniably, it lacks the *élan* of that of the 1890s.

Moorcrag, Gillhead, near Cartmel Fell, Windermere, of 1898-99, which followed shortly after Broadleys, was built for JW Buckley. The contract drawings for the house were witnessed by Thomas H Mawson, who was to design the garden for Moorcrag. Mawson is an interesting figure in his own right. He was to become the first lecturer in landscape design in Britain, at Liverpool University; his *Art and Craft of Garden Making*, London, 1900, is an excellent work which has been rather overlooked by garden historians, mesmerised by Gertrude Jeckyll. A house by Mawson, which is illustrated in his book, suggests the influence of Voysey.

Moorcrag, unlike Greyfriars and Broadleys, is a rather informal, even modest, house – the entrance has a space for bicycles. Despite its intimacy, Moorcrag is compositionally satisfying and must be numbered among Voysey's most successful houses.

In 1899 Voysey was commissioned to design a house by HG Wells (1866-1946). Wells was not at all enthusiastic about the typical Voysey heart on the front door. Voysey simply added a stalk and the heart became a spade – hence Spade House. Both men would have enjoyed the joke and the symbolism of the spade which traditionally has the same meaning as the hoe – the implement with which Adam tilled the Garden of Eden. It is a symbol of Spring.

At 33, Wells had already established a fairly considerable reputation with *The Time Machine* (1895), *The Island of Doctor Moreau* (1896), *The Invisible Man* (1897) and *The War of the Worlds* (1898). If the epithet 'avant-garde' is not quite applicable to him, 'progressive' certainly is. Spade House, near Folkestone in Kent, was built on a sloping site – rather like that of New Place – a house for another literary figure, AMM Stedman, the publisher. Wells was to write *Kipps* (1905), *The War in the Air* (1908), *Tono Bungay* (1909) and *The History of Mr Polly* (1910) at Spade House.

The close contact which Wells had with Voysey during its design evidently inspired an interest in architecture. In *Kipps*, Book Three, The Housing Question, Wells describes the design of Kipps' house. Although Kipps' architect, with his cynical attitude over the matter of style, does not remotely resemble Voysey, Wells' description of how he made careful notes on his client's exact requirements does suggest Voysey. So too does his account of 'a small, alert individual', who sat 'with his hat and his bag exactly equidistant right and left'. The well-known photograph of Voysey in his study at The Orchard, Chorley Wood, with his papers neatly arranged in front of him, suggests that he was similarly meticulous to the point of obsessiveness.

Kipps' architect wanted to see a site plan in order that he could decide where to put the 'ugly side' of the house. Many Victorian houses had an ugly side or more often three. There was never an ugly side to a Voysey House.

Life in Spade House is described by MM Meyer, the Swiss governess of the Wells family, in *HG Wells and his Family*, London, 1955. Miss Meyer spoke of the beautiful garden and the 'homelike and unpretentious atmosphere' of Spade House. It is indeed an unpretentious house and typically Voysey. But it does not induce quite the same *frisson* of delight which Greyfriars or Broadleys do. An extra floor was added to the house in 1903, by Voysey, which has not had the devastating effect of the barbarous alterations to Greyfriars.

In the same year as he worked on Spade House, Voysey began work on the design of a house for his own family – The Orchard, Chorley Wood, Hertfordshire. He had just moved his office to Baker Street, conveniently situated near Marylebone Station, the

London terminus of the Metropolitan Line which led to Chorley Wood. He became, in fact, a commuter. The Orchard represented, in material terms, a fairly considerable degree of success.

Voysey's own house, The Orchard, should be worthy of discussion. It is a typical Voysey House though less remarkable than Moorcrag which was not very much larger. The largest room, the dining room, is 15 foot by 20 foot. There is no sitting room, merely the often illustrated hall, with its small fireplace. There is no room which Mrs Voysey could have really considered her own.

While the Voysey marriage never completely foundered, husband and wife drew further apart as time went on. Increasingly, Voysey was to live on his own. At 60, when most men have come to depend upon the comforts associated with married life, he moved into a flat in St James' Street. He lived and worked there until a few months before his death, in Winchester – on February 12, 1941.

During the first five years of the 20th century Voysey was to design a number of houses. None had quite the authority of his best houses of the 1890s – the Forster house, Perrycroft, Greyfriars, Broadleys or Moorcrag.

Among the houses of this period are: Prior's Garth, near Puttenham, Surrey, 1900; The Pastures, North Luffenham, Leicestershire, 1901; Vodin, Pyrford, Surrey, 1902; Ty Bronna, Fairwater, near Cardiff, 1903; White Cottage, Wimbledon, 1903; Tilehurst, Bushey, Hertfordshire, 1903; Hollybank, Chorley Wood, 1903 – which was very near to The Orchard; Myholme, Bushey, Hertfordshire, 1904; Hollymount, Knotty Green, Beaconsfield, Buckinghamshire, 1905; and The Homestead, Frinton-on-Sea, Essex, 1905.

The Pastures and The Homestead are the most memorable of these turn-of-the-century houses. The former has something of the look of the 19th-century model farm about it. There is half-timbering above the doors of the carriage-house which is reminiscent of Voysey's earlier houses such as the unbuilt cottage of 1885 and Walnut Tree Farm of 1890. Voysey always proceeded by small steps and never by quantum leaps. He intended the house to be built of stone from the locality but it is said that he was over-ruled by his client. Cost, no doubt, was the deciding factor.

The Homestead, Frinton-on-Sea is an entirely typical Voysey House. There are no major features about it which are not found in earlier houses. Nevertheless, it affirms the validity of the Voysey method. Contemporary photographs of the interiors show an austere house but Voysey seems closer to the Puritan ideal than he does to proto-modernity.

In 1902, Voysey designed what was to be his only industrial building, a factory for A Sanderson & Sons, the wallpaper manufacturers, in Chiswick, a West London suburb. It has been much illustrated and frequently discussed. Pevsner called it 'a clean and charming design'. It is clad externally with white glazed tiles – an idea which Voysey probably borrowed from Halsey Ricardo, another, though rather unorthodox, Arts and Crafts architect. Ricardo believed passionately that the external surfaces of buildings should be easily washable.

Compositionally the factory is very strong and it compares favourably in this respect with some of Voysey's best houses of the 1890s. Bands of low arched windows, like those found in early 19th-century South of England water-mills, are located within a simple grid defined by prominent buttresses. At first sight, these buttresses appear to be a medievalising feature but they in fact ingeniously conceal ventilating ducts. They terminate with the rather exaggerated, flattened caps which Voysey occasionally used on his furniture – like those on the bedposts on the double bed in The Orchard, or a dresser of 1898 which was shown in the exhibition *CFA Voysey: Architect and Designer 1857-1941*, Brighton Pavilion, 1978. These caps appear to derive from those which were to be found on the upright members of the small timber Century Guild exhibition stand which his friend AH Mackmurdo designed for an exhibition of 1886. The deep parapet, which links

*ABOVE*: MOORCRAG, 1898; *BELOW*: BEDROOM, GARDEN CORNER, LONDON, 1908

the buttresses, curves elegantly – like the foot of The Orchard bed and the dresser and, indeed, the top of the Century Guild stand. Nevertheless, one does not for a moment think of the factory as merely a scaled-up piece of furniture.

Built on a claustrophobic site, the Sanderson factory, although it cannot be seen as a totality, as in Voysey's perspective, makes a dramatic impact. With very considerable skill, Voysey designed a building which possesses precisely those architectonic qualities that can be enjoyed from the restricted viewpoint of the very narrow access road.

A wallpaper factory does not call for great chimneys, or tall assembly sheds – for wallpaper making was, in the early years of the century, a craft. Voysey would have had been in particular sympathy with the Sandersons who were long-standing purchasers of his wallpaper designs. What would Voysey have made of designing factories for heavy industrial processes, as Hans Poelzig was to do very shortly after the Sanderson exercise?

Voysey was 49 in 1906. At the time it seemed that if all went well, he could have looked forward to at least another twenty or so years of work, like his father, who, at 78, was still preaching the optimistic, if not anodyne, message of Theism.

A mere 20 more years of designing would have taken Voysey right up to the time of what is so often said to have been the first real manifestation of the International Style – the *Pavillon de l'Esprit Nouveau* at the *Exposition Internationale des Arts Décoratifs* in Paris in 1925, by Le Corbusier.

There were to be only eight years left of practice. Voysey's career as a fully-fledged architect, someone, that is, sustained primarily by an architectural practice, was not a very lengthy one at just a little over a quarter of a century. Nothing like as long as the careers of William Butterfield, or Richard Norman Shaw, or Lutyens. To say nothing of Van de Velde, or Josef Hoffmann.

The outbreak of the Great War, in August 1914, effectively brought Voysey's career as an architect to an end. He continued until the 1930s, with at best only modest financial success, to design fabrics, carpets and wallpapers. But, however accomplished he was at these activities, they did not bring him the intellectual elation which architecture did.

Voysey's architectural career can be divided conveniently into four stages: the first, 1888-91, the stage during which he devised a highly individual architectural vocabulary; the second, 1892-95, when he was perfecting this vocabulary; the third, 1896-1905, the mature and most brilliant phase – when he designed Greyfriars and Broadleys; and the fourth, 1906-14, which should have been one been of consolidation. It is this stage which concerns us now. What did Voysey achieve between 1906 and 1914?

These years are, frankly, disappointing for anyone who admires Voysey. There is a certain lack of rigour in his work. His inventiveness seems to have been in eclipse – Pevsner and Nairn, remember, had written of how Voysey could make 'clichés out of his style'. He was possibly less fortunate with his clients than he had been in the late 1890s. This is not to say that Voysey lacked clients during these years. Far from it: in many ways his practice flourished. But sophisticated and sympathetic clients – like Julian Russell Sturgis of Greyfriars, or Currer Briggs of Broadleys – were harder to find.

A look at any of the many Edwardian books on the middle class house will show that new talents were emerging such as WH Bidlake, Walter H Brierley, E Guy Dawber, RS Lorimer, Mervyn Macartney, Barry Parker and Raymond Unwin, Robert Weir Schultz, Charles Spooner and Leonard Stokes. Then there were such men as Baillie Scott, who published an excellent and influential manual *Houses and Gardens*, in 1906.

Waiting in the wings was Lutyens, who seems to have been making the running in popular house books. (Five shillings or seven and sixpence a copy and illustrated with plans and excellent photographs.) By 1906 Voysey must have seemed no more than a talented architect among many.

Besides the fierce competition which Voysey faced as a result of the sheer numbers of more than competent designers of middle-class houses – an *embarras de richesse* if ever there was one – there was also the matter of style. A glance through any of the mid-Edwardian house books will reveal that Voysey, in terms of style, was somewhat isolated.

Baillie Scott, for all the underlying logicality of his architecture, favoured a more seductively picturesque approach than Voysey. Lutyens understood exactly how paraphrases of vernacular details could be surreptitiously employed to display wealth. (Only on one occasion, in 1897, with the unfortunate front elevation of Norney Grange, can Voysey ever have been said to have resorted to display for its own sake.) Furthermore, Lutyens was increasingly turning towards Palladianism. Other contemporaries, too, like Stokes, or Brierley, were also drawn to forms of classicism, if more eclectic and less forcefully expressed.

The Voysey style had probably been over-exposed. For ten years or so, Voysey had figured very prominently in *The Studio* and in its European equivalents. Voysey, who once reaped the benefits of fashionable taste, was now himself falling victim to its vagaries.

A list of Voysey's completed projects between 1906 and 1914 does not suggest, for a moment, that he was running out of clients. But none of these clients wanted from Voysey what he was demonstrably best at – the middle-sized country house built on a fine site such as Perrycroft, Greyfriars, Broadleys and Moorcrag.

Among the more important of the projects from 1906 until the outbreak of the Great War were : the remodelling of offices for the Essex and Suffolk Equitable Insurance Company, New Broad Street, London EC1, 1906-10; Littleholme, Guildford, for G Muntzer, 1906-07; another Littleholme, this time at Kendal, for AW Simpson, 1909; Lodge Style, Combe Down, for T Sturge Cotterell, 1909; a house in Belfast, Northern Ireland, for Robert Hetherington, 1911; and the Pleasure Ground, Kensal Green, London W10, for EJ Horniman, 1913. Muntzer and EJ Horniman had been long-standing clients. Voysey designed fabrics for Muntzer and had designed Lowicks, near Frensham, for Horniman, in 1894.

Of these projects, Littleholme, Kendal, for AM Simpson is the most noteworthy. Simpson was a discerning craftsman, designer and furniture maker. The name must have been suggested by Voysey. It is surely too much of a coincidence that two clients, Muntzer and Simpson, quite independently of each other decided to call their houses such a mawkish name.

Littleholme is small, with 24-inch thick walls of local stone. The stone is left, unlike neighbouring Broadleys or Moorcrag, exposed. Windows are small and the house has an austere air about it.

At a fleeting glance, Littleholme might be seen, because of its studied simplicity, as an early manifestation of modernism. This would be quite wrong. It is an Arts and Crafts house. Idiosyncratic, with its overscale but beautifully detailed porch, Littleholme must be regarded as one of Voysey's most successful houses.

An oddity, but also worthy of discussion, is Lodge Style also of 1909. The house is built of dressed stone as the client T Sturge Cotterell owned a quarry in the locality and wanted to supply his own stone. It is said that the eccentric Cotterell wanted a single-storey house – one hesitates to call it a bungalow – which resembled, as far as was possible on a miniature scale, Merton College, Oxford. Lodge Style was built around a college courtyard. With the exception of the arched porch, which was exactly like that at The Pastures, of 1901, Lodge Style would almost pass as a Gothic Revival parish school of the 1840s.

In 1914 Voysey returned again to the Gothic Revival language that he had learned in the office of Seddon in the 1870s. His competition entry for the City of Ottawa Government Buildings was in a late-medieval or Tudor style. Its mullioned windows bear a resemblance to those of such buildings as the Charterhouse at Finsbury, which largely dates from the late 16th century. Voysey, it might be remembered, had much earlier demonstrated a fondness for Tudor details with his design for The Cottage of around 1885. The same might be said for the Teignmouth Sanatorium of 1884.

The Ottawa Government Buildings possess an unhappy mechanical quality which can be seen all too often in very late Gothic Revival architecture. It can be observed in Gilbert Scott's Liverpool Cathedral, as well as Charles Rennie Mackintosh's rejected designs for the same cathedral of 1903 which, for all their brilliant massing, are lifeless and unconvincing. Medieval architecture was extemporised and organic, as few but Ruskin truly understood. Voysey merely fails where his peers failed. This is not, however, to say the Arts and Crafts solution had failed.

At the outbreak of war in 1914, Voysey had three schemes for houses in hand. These were: a house at Wilmslow, Cheshire, for his brother, the Reverend EA Voysey; a largish and a rather fussy house at Ashmansworth, Berkshire; and a house at Thatcham Coldash, Berkshire. None of the projects was revived after the war.

All that Voysey actually built after the war were war memorials. One was constructed at Malvern Wells, Hereford in 1919, and the other at Potter's Bar, Hertfordshire, in 1920. There were also alterations to a house owned by AH Van Gruisen in Hambledon, Surrey, of 1919, and the re-modelling of a room in 29 Harley Street, London W1, for Leslie Paton, also in 1919.

Three post-war projects fell through. None, in truth, would have enhanced Voysey's reputation. These were a flat-roofed house with battlements, at Laughton, near Market Harborough, of 1920; a house at St Nicholas-at-Wade, Kent; and a large house, designed with dull symmetrical elevations for Carl Löw in 1922, to be built in Czechoslovakia. Voysey's only other overseas project seems to have been a house for a Dr Leigh Canney at Aswan, Egypt, of 1905, which photographs confirm was actually built.

In 1923 Voysey proposed a scheme for three identical residential tower blocks, with communal restaurants, for a site in Piccadilly which had become vacant because of the demolition of Devonshire House. The idea arose out of a competition organised to find an appropriate use for the site. The tower blocks are of 30 storeys and have light wells in their centres which would have been ineffective in dispersing light at the lower levels. At the corner of each of the blocks is an emergency staircase which is treated as a keep in a Norman castle. The blocks were taller than anything London knew at the time and show the unexpected influence of the North American skyscraper, These must have furnished Voysey with the idea of the tall building with medieval details. Voysey must surely have known of the work of such skyscraper architects as Warren and Wetmore through periodicals.

With the decline of his practice, Voysey went through a very lean time financially. This continued for many years, up to the end of his life. On April 17, 1918, he wrote to his friend Alexander Morton, the Carlisle textile manufacturer and a long-standing patron, of his 'terrible plight – could you give me anything to do?'

On April 26, 1929, he wrote to Morton again : 'I am in terribly low water and distracted by financial worry – I have not so much as sixty pounds left. No one will commission an architect of seventy-two'. In a postscript to a letter to Morton of June 11, he remarked : 'The Council of the RIBA have elected me a full Fellow, a compliment which will not prevent me from starving.'

Another letter to Morton, written a few days later, on June 19, 1929, reveals Voysey's pathetic situation:

> I must tell you that the manager of the Wallpaper Manufacturers Ltd told me yesterday that the retaining fee of £200 *per annum* must cease at the end of August next. But he added if I could induce the Weavers and Cotton Printers to contribute toward the retainer his company might consider contributing too. It is very painful to me to go begging on my own behalf.

> . . PS Without that £200 I should have to leave my flat, sell all my furniture and bury myself in a slum.

With no fees from architecture and barely a pittance to be earned from designing wallpapers and textiles – and that by no means secure – Voysey had fallen on hard times. There was no private money, as far as one knows. He appears to have retained little or nothing from his days of successful practice. The war years had probably eaten up what capital he had.

In the early 20s, when a flaccid neo-Georgianism prevailed, Voysey's architecture must have seemed as *passé* as *The Yellow Book* – that symbol of the 90s. Yet, unexpectedly, Voysey's reputation was to be revived in the 1930s.

The rehabilitation of Voysey appears to have first begun with a series of five anonymous articles in *The Architect* and *Building News* in 1927. The restoration of Voysey's reputation continued with a retrospective exhibition, at the Batsford Gallery in 1931. It was not until 1934 that William Morris was accorded a similar honour.

The Voysey exhibition evidently created something of a stir. It inspired the young John Betjeman to write about him in 'Charles Francis Annesley Voysey. The Architect of Individualism', *The Architectural Review*, LXX, 1931, pp 93-96.

Betjeman observed in his short article:

> Only in England is Voysey not taken at his true value, for he is dismissed as art nouveau or even 'arty' . . . The sincerity of Voysey's architecture refutes all slurs that it is deliberately unusual . . . To him aesthetic and moral values are inseparable . . . since he is an individualist, he considers the training of character to be of far greater importance than any knowledge of styles and books . . . Although we see many of his decorative details reproduced *ad nauseam* in the tea shop, waiting room and monster furnishing store, the simplicity to which he – as much if not more than William Morris – leads us back from the complex and futile revivalism, in which many architects still remain, has made itself felt at least on the continent.

Thus Betjeman – uncharacteristically perhaps – connects Voysey with the Modern Movement. It is not entirely easy to dismiss the connection, if one subscribes to that familiar but mythologising view of history which, in its naively Darwinian way, saw the history of architecture culminating, triumphing, in the Modern Movement. And try as we might to cast it aside, parts of this history still linger in our collective unconscious.

This same connection between Voysey and the Modern Movement is also assumed by Raymond McGrath in *Twentieth Century Houses* (London 1934), a readable Modern Movement primer evidently aimed at a wide audience.[1] Because of its historical interest, it deserves to be better known.

Besides Voysey, McGrath elevates other architects to the status of pioneer proto-Moderns. These include: Charles Ashbee, Charles Rennie Mackintosh, George Walton, Baillie Scott and his later partner Edward Beresford, as well as, Adams Holden and Pearson, and, most unexpectedly of all, Sir Giles Gilbert Scott, who is represented by a commonplace neo-Georgian house.[2]

'We rightly put Ashbee, Voysey, Mackintosh and Walton first in order among the architects of the last thirty years,' wrote McGrath, 'not because of the value of the buildings produced by them, but because they did much of our hard work for us.' This is the archetypical Moderno-centric view which began to be questioned more than a couple of decades ago.

Nikolaus Pevsner, in his *Pioneers of Modern Design*, which first appeared in 1936 with a title which indicated its leitmotif. *Pioneers of the Modern Movement* made more references to Voysey than he did to any other 'pioneer'. Pevsner says of Voysey, when writing of Broadleys, the Windermere house of 1898:

> Here . . . was a mind equally averse to the picturesque tricks of the Shaw school and the preciousness of Art Nouveau.

From [its] centre bay with its completely unmoulded mullions and transoms, from these windows cut clean and sheer into the wall, access to the architectural style of today could have been direct . . .

The case of Voysey was a particularly infuriating one for historians of the Modern Movement. If only Voysey had been able to make that leap – such a small leap – to Modernity.

Reyner Banham, in *Theory and Design in the First Machine Age*, published first in 1960, has things to say about Voysey too:

> . . . it is common knowledge that Voysey's own intention was only to improve and continue the native cottage vernacular of Southern England. He had no conception of the importance of what he was doing (he seems to have had the almost pathological modesty of some English provincial intellectuals) and angrily deprecated any attempt to link his name with the Modern Movement. Under the circumstances it should not surprise us that his practices and aims should be at variance with one another. His work excels by the sharp definition of one smooth plain surface from another, the fine precision of his arises and the bold geometry of his forms, and yet he was quoted in 1906 as saying that he preferred: 'The soft effect of the outline of an old building where the angles were put up by eye, compared with the mechanical effect of the modern drafted style.'

Banham, like McGrath, or Pevsner, had all dutifully followed the Modernist line. But who in 1960, apart from John Brandon-Jones, who is part of the Arts and Crafts apostolic succession, would have dared to say otherwise?

It is not the wrongness of McGrath's, Pevsner's, or Banham's views which strikes one – for being wrong on some counts at least is the just prerogative of the best historians – but the fact that Voysey's *oeuvre* is valued principally as representing an interim stage between the Arts and Crafts Movement and the Modern Movement. Voysey was the representative of an inventive and autonomous architectural culture. He must be judged as such.

Towards the end of Voysey's career the honours came. In 1924, at the age of 67, he was made Master of the Art Workers' Guild, which to the present day has staunchly defended the values of the Arts and Crafts. In 1936 he was one of the earliest designers to be honoured with the title 'Designer for Industry' by the Royal Society of Arts. In 1940, probably too late for him to savour fully, he was awarded his greatest honour – the gold Medal of the Royal Institute of British Architects. At the beginning of a vile war Voysey's innocence and his unfailing belief in art seemed impossibly remote from the realities of the 20th century. For Voysey, who had grown to maturity during the 1880s, when bourgeois Aestheticism erupted, believed in art as passionately as Walter Pater, but without Pater's hedonism. Art was an entirely benign and therapeutic power for Voysey – as it had been for William Morris.

Might it still be just a little too early to evaluate Voysey's achievements? For if a 'green' school develops, his architecture will be studied with the utmost seriousness. One can say with conviction that he has become a myth not unlike Roland Barthes' Eiffel Tower. Who else, among British architects, has attained mythic status? Possibly Inigo Jones, Wren, Hawksmoor, Adam, Soane, Pugin, Butterfield, Shaw, and Lutyens. But Voysey is more ordinary and less remote than all of these. He is the most approachable of great architects. This is his achievement.

## Notes

1 Raymond McGrath, 1903-77, an Australian, did some interesting work in the 1930s; he was co-ordinator of the successful interior schemes for the BBC's Broadcasting House and the designer of an adventurous, part-circular, house of 1937 at Chertsey in Surrey.

2 Incidentally, FRS Yorke in *The Modern House in England*, London, 1937, ilustrates houses by the following precursors of the Modern Movement: Philip Webb's The Red House, 1859; Voysey's The Orchard, 1900; and Mackintosh's Hill House, Helensburgh, 1902-03. Yorke's real Moderns are: Peter Behrens, Thomas S Tait, Amyas Connell, George Checkley and Colin Lucas.

HOLLYBANK UNDER CONSTRUCTION WITH THE ORCHARD IN BACKGROUND, 1903

# COTTAGE FOR MR AND MRS CFA VOYSEY, 1885
## *UNEXECUTED DESIGN*

*The cottage has some affinities with the work of George Devey (1820-86), the country house designer, for whom Voysey worked for nearly two years. In this design one can also detect the influence of Richard Norman Shaw, whose half-timbered Merrist Wood (1870), in Surrey, Voysey may well have seen.*

*Running contrary to the notion of a medieval style*

*country dwelling, the spaces between the cottage's tarred timbers were to be filled in with concrete. In order to economise the brick walls were thin but buttressed for strength. The ground floor was to be covered in white painted roughcast. The cottage is the first example of the Voysey House. It was illustrated in* The Studio *and* Dekorative Kunst.

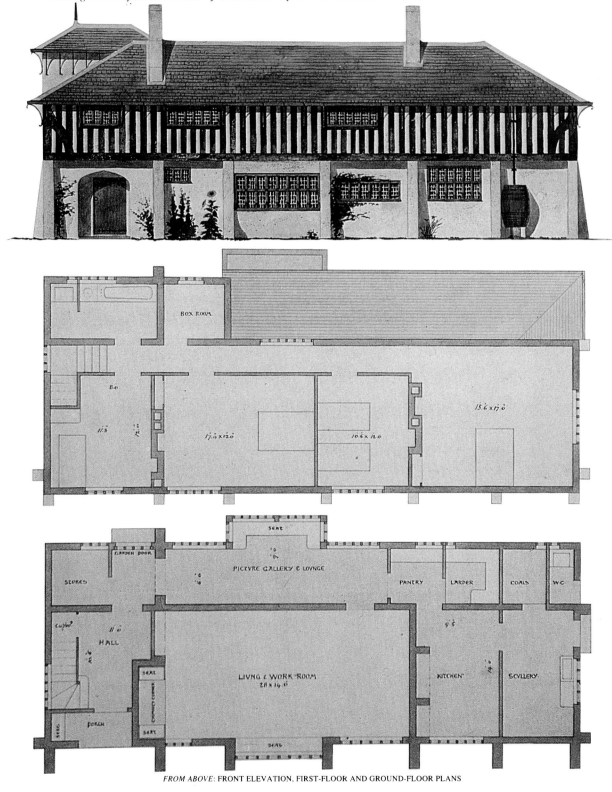

*FROM ABOVE:* FRONT ELEVATION, FIRST-FLOOR AND GROUND-FLOOR PLANS

# AN ARTIST'S COTTAGE, 1894
## *UNEXECUTED DESIGN*

*This project clearly once again demonstrates the main influences upon Voysey – after, of course, his early Gothic Revival mentor, JP Seddon – George Devey and Richard Norman Shaw. The Devey influence is seen in the neo-vernacular aspects of the building and its relaxed agglomeration of parts. The Shaw influence is* *less obvious at a glance. However, the exposed-brick studio is decidedly reminiscent of studio houses built by Shaw. Voysey, of course, like his contemporaries would have been fully conversant with Shaw's work; besides, he had in 1891 built a studio house in Bedford Park, which was principally designed by Shaw.*

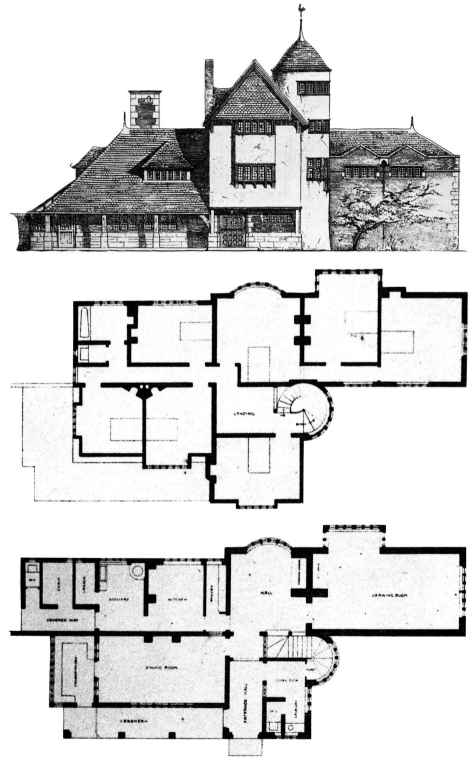

*FROM ABOVE*: FRONT ELEVATION, FIRST-FLOOR AND GROUND-FLOOR PLANS

# 14 SOUTH PARADE, 1891
## *BEDFORD PARK, LONDON W4*

*This has some affinities with the unexecuted 'tower house' designs which were published in* British Architect, XXXI, *in 1889. The house which could be seen by middle-class commuters on the District Line, served to publicise Voysey's ideas. By comparing it with the* adjoining pair of red-brick houses by Richard Norman Shaw, Voysey's authentic radicalism will become immediately apparent. Despite its advanced design, it represents a logical continuation of Gothic Revival practices.*

*OPPOSITE*: RECENT VIEW OF GARDEN FRONT; *ABOVE*: EDWARDIAN VIEW OF GARDEN FRONT

# COTTAGE, 1888
## *BISHOP'S ITCHINGTON, WARWICKSHIRE*

*Although the half-timbering of the unexecuted cottage of 1885 has been omitted, apparently for reasons of economy, this cottage has a good deal in common with the earlier design. The Cottage for MH Lakin has* *features in common with Gothic Revival parsonages by such architects as Butterfield or JP Seddon. It was illustrated in* British Architect, XXX, *1888, and would have helped to publicise Voysey's ideas.*

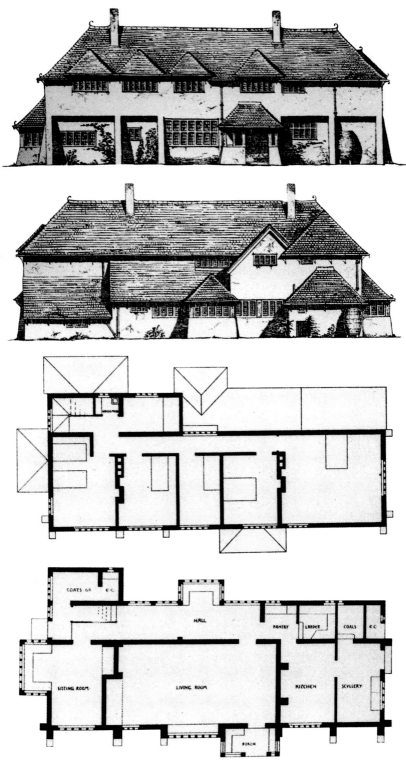

*FROM ABOVE*: FRONT AND REAR ELEVATIONS; FIRST-FLOOR AND GROUND-FLOOR PLANS

# WALNUT TREE FARM, 1890
## *CASTLEMORTON, MALVERN*

*The house is L-shaped, with the service wing – kitchen and scullery – deprived of the view of the garden. (Voysey, and presumably his client, had strong views about the status of servants.) Voysey uses a similar arrangement in one of his finest houses, Broadleys, Lake Windermere, 1898. The three main rooms – 'best parlour', living-room and morning-room – are interconnected. Because of restrictive local by-laws the* timbering above the dormers could not be structural. Voysey abandoned timbering of this bogus kind in subsequent houses.

*W Alexander Harvey, who was to design many houses in Bourneville, an early garden suburb in Birmingham, produced a paraphrase of this house, which was illustrated in* The Studio *in 1903. Walnut Tree Farm was illustrated in* British Architect, XXXIV, *1890.*

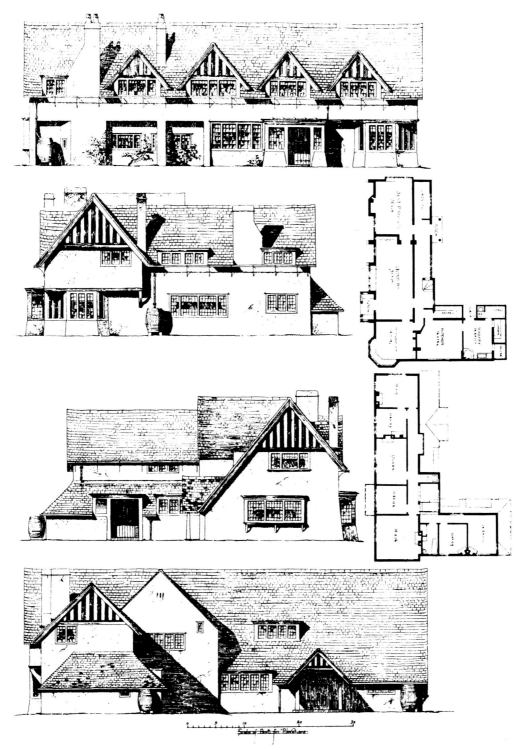

*ABOVE*: ELEVATIONS AND PLANS

*ABOVE*: SIDE VIEW; *BELOW*: DRAWING OF INTERIOR

*ABOVE AND BELOW:* VIEW AND DRAWING OF GARDEN FRONT

# STUDIO HOUSE, 1891
## ST DUNSTAN'S ROAD, LONDON W6

The house was designed as both studio and living quarters for the artist WEF Britten. The dual function of the house is reflected in the design. The studio proper, at the rear, resembles an industrial building with its hammered plate-glass roof lights. The roof of the porch is supported by wooden brackets, each incorporating a silhouette profile which is apparently Voysey's (such a joke reflects the medievalism often lurking in Voysey's thinking). In contrast, the wrought-iron railings are quite unique to this urban commission. The buttressing of the chimneys, stone mullions and projecting eaves, supported by iron brackets, roughcast finish and characteristically Voysean proportions, make the studio an oddity in an otherwise conventional Victorian Street.

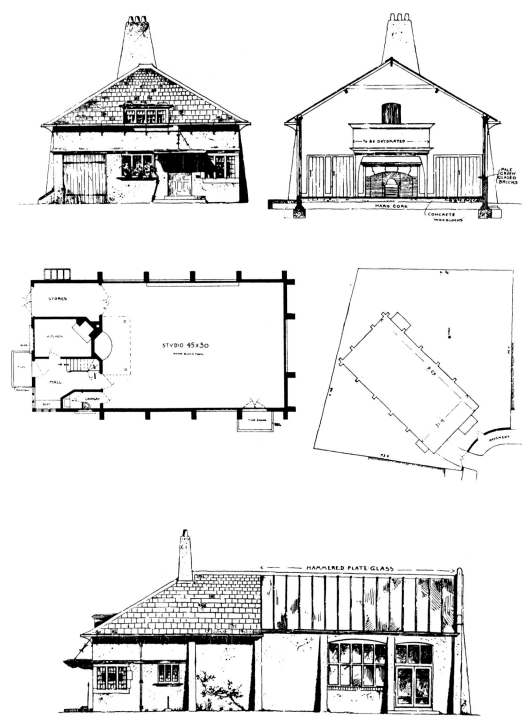

*ABOVE*: FRONT ELEVATION AND SECTION; *MIDDLE*: GROUND-FLOOR AND SITE PLANS; *BELOW*: SIDE OR WEST ELEVATION

# THE HANS ROAD HOUSES, 1892
## *KNIGHTSBRIDGE, LONDON SW3*

*These are Voysey's only town houses. An 1891 scheme for a terrace of houses in Swan Walk, Chelsea, had been abandoned. Voysey uses the same dark red brick favoured by Richard Norman Shaw for his Queen Anne style houses built in the area roughly a decade earlier. An adjoining, clumsily classicising house by Voysey's former friend AH Mackmurdo makes a telling contrast.*

*Originally there were to have been three houses by*

*Voysey, but he fell out with his client over fee. Mackmurdo was selected as architect for the third house and their friendship was ended.*

*Bold rainwater pipes – more chastely deployed in the facades of well-mannered Aesthetic Movement houses – formed a distinctive feature of the original design. Julian Russell Sturgis, the novelist – for whom Voysey was to design Greyfriars in 1897 – lived in no 16.*

*ABOVE:* DRAWING OF 14 & 16 HANS ROAD

*ABOVE*: VIEW OF HANS ROAD

*ABOVE*: INTERIOR; *BELOW*: DRAWING SHOWING DOORS WITH HEART MOTIF

*ABOVE*: VIEW OF HOUSE

# PERRYCROFT, 1893
## *COLWALL, NEAR MALVERN*

A substantial and expensive house which cost nearly £5000 – a very large sum at the time. Perrycroft was Voysey's first important commission. It was widely publicised and appeared in the first European article on Voysey in Dekorative Kunst I, 1897. The walls are of brick with a roughcast finish. Perrycroft can be seen as a precursor of Voysey's two finest houses, Greyfriars, 1897 and Broadleys, 1898. However, a certain residual fussiness is to be observed and it does not possess the austere intellectuality of the two later houses.

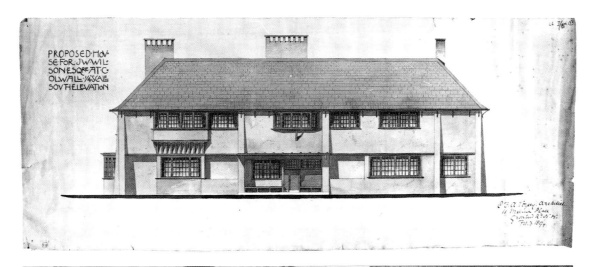

*ABOVE*: SOUTH ELEVATION; *BELOW*: ORIGINAL INTERIOR

*ABOVE*: VIEW FROM NORTH; *BELOW*: VIEW FROM SOUTH

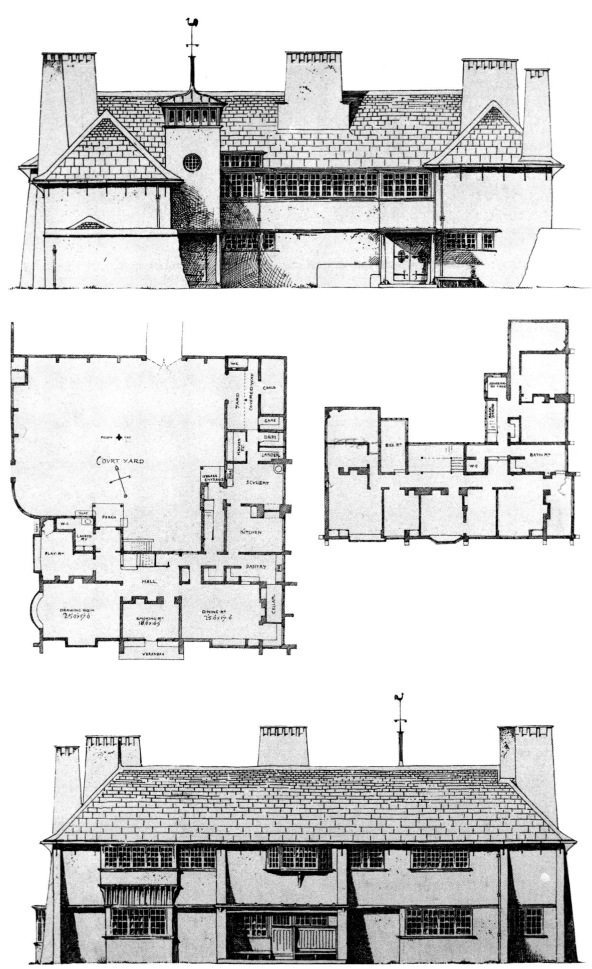

*ABOVE*: NORTH ELEVATION; *MIDDLE*: GROUND-FLOOR AND FIRST-FLOOR PLANS; *BELOW*: SOUTH ELEVATION

*ABOVE*: VIEW OF GARDEN FRONT

# LOWICKS, 1894
## *FRENSHAM, SURREY*

*The house was designed for EJ Horniman, who was a member of the wealthy tea-importing family. There is a half-timbered dormer set above a band of windows which is an engaging feature. Lutyens was to use similar bands of windows in early houses such as Munstead Wood, near Godalming, which was built for Gertrude Jekyll, the landscape gardener, in 1896.*

*Like many of Voysey's early clients, the Horniman family had intellectual interests. Lowicks foreshadows the houses of Voysey's mature phase.*

*ABOVE*: ILLUSTRATION OF HOUSE INCLUDING GROUND-FLOOR AND FIRST-FLOOR PLANS; *BELOW*: RECENT VIEW OF GARDEN FRONT

*ABOVE*: VIEW FROM THE SOUTH; *BELOW*: VIEW SHOWING ENTRANCE

# ANNESLEY LODGE, 1895
## *PLATT'S LANE, HAMPSTEAD*

The house is L-shaped like the earlier Walnut Tree Farm. Here however, the main entrance is placed at the intersection of the two wings creating a new kind of monumentality. One could argue that the Lodge is, in fact, a precursor of the 'butterfly plan' – a house type which was in mode during the 1900s.

Annesley Lodge was designed for Voysey's father, the Rev Charles Voysey, who had been left a legacy by George Devey, one of Voysey's mentors. It is possible that this legacy paid for the house.

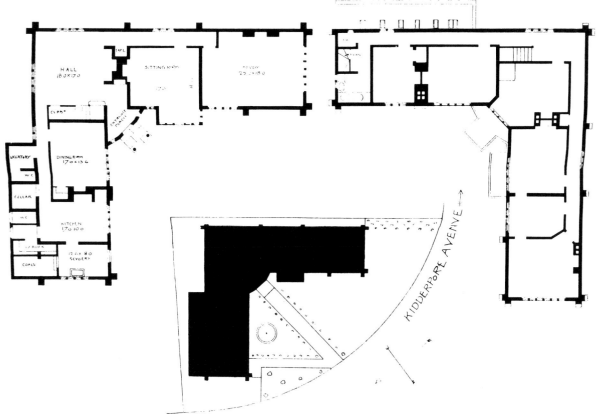

ABOVE: DRAWING; *MIDDLE*: GROUND-FLOOR AND FIRST-FLOOR PLANS; *BELOW*: SITE PLAN

*ABOVE*: INTERIOR; *BELOW*: SOUTH-WEST ELEVATION

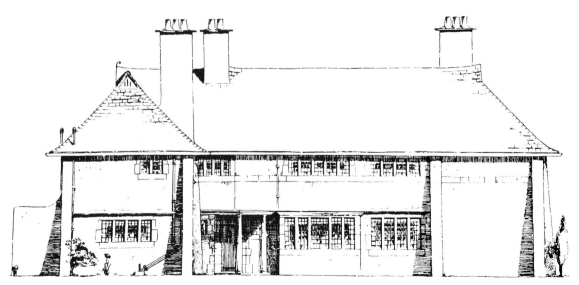

*ABOVE*: INTERIOR; *BELOW*: NORTH-WEST ELEVATION

# GREYFRIARS, 1896
## *HOG'S BACK, SURREY*

*The dramatic sweep of the roof and the stone-mullioned bay were perhaps the most prominent features of this beautifully situated house. However, the roof line was tampered with in H Baker's unsympathetic alterations of 1913. Dormers were also added at this time and the original dazzling simplicity – never to be confused with* Proto-Modernity *– was obscured. The client's perspective by H Gaye was reproduced many times and in photographic form the house appeared in Hermann Muthesius'* Das Englische Haus *of 1904-05. Greyfriars can be claimed to be among the most influential of Voysey's houses. It is certainly one of his best.*

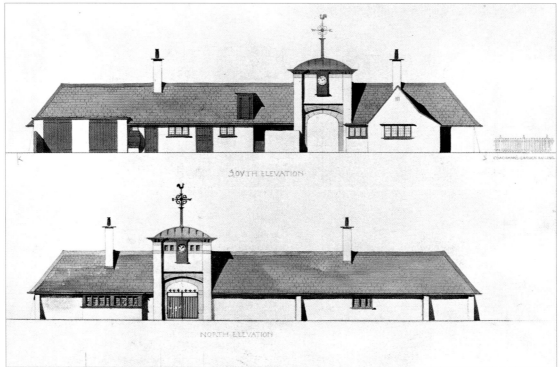

*ABOVE*: ILLUSTRATION OF HOUSE INCLUDING GROUND-FLOOR AND FIRST-FLOOR PLANS; *BELOW*: NORTH AND SOUTH ELEVATIONS OF THE STABLES

# NEW PLACE, 1897
## *HASLEMERE, SURREY*

*New Place was designed for AAM Stedman, later Sir Algernon Methuen, the very successful publisher. Though complex in form and outline, it has none of the deficiencies of Norney. Voysey exploits the sloping site with very great skill. This he does without over dramatising* *it but by making the ground's gradation seem the most natural thing in the world through the creation of different levels and terracing. There is a large bell at the apex of the roof above the garden entrance which was tolled to call the family in for meals.*

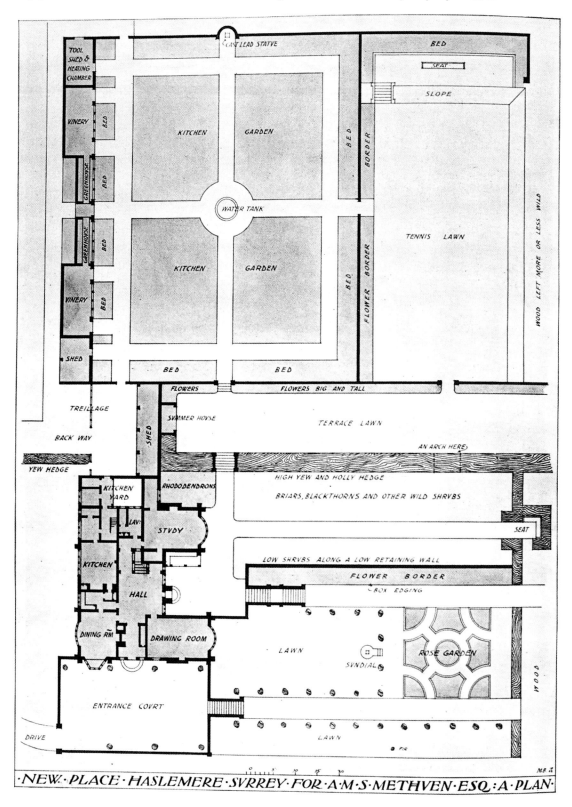

ABOVE: PLAN SHOWING THE RELATION OF THE HOUSE TO THE GARDEN

*ABOVE AND BELOW*: GARDEN AND ENTRANCE FRONTS

*ABOVE AND BELOW*: INTERIOR VIEWS

*ABOVE*: VIEW OF GARDEN FRONT; *BELOW*: SIDE OR SOUTH-EAST ELEVATION

# NORNEY, 1897
## *SHACKLEFORD, SURREY*

*Although the garden elevation is by no means unsuccessful, the front elevation has an awkward asymmetry. The front entrance has that over-worked, over didactic, quality sometimes found in the houses of Philip Webb –* *in Clouds, Knoyle, for example.*

*Voysey's client Rev Leighton Crane was a wealthy, artistically inclined, clergyman – by no means an unusual 19th-century phenomenon.*

*ABOVE*: NORTH-EAST ELEVATION; *BELOW*: HALL INTERIOR

# BROADLEYS, 1898
## *LAKE WINDERMERE, CUMBRIA*

*One of Voysey's finest houses, designed as a holiday home for A Currer Briggs, the son of a Yorkshire colliery owner. Compositionally, the elevation with its three bow windows overlooking the lake is particularly successful. At first glance, it may be read as symmetrical. But the arrangement of the chimneys and the presence of the porthole-like window to the right of the central bay show a Gothic contempt for the easy and* *meretricious option of symmetry.*

*Near contemporary photographs (such as those in Hermann Muthesius' Das Englische Haus, 1904-05) show Broadley's as it was designed by Voysey. Unfortunately, the custom-made furniture has long since been dispersed. (As an old man, it is said that Voysey would never revisit one of his houses if his original interiors had not been retained.)*

*OPPOSITE*: CLOSE-UP OF BOW WINDOWS ON LAKE FRONT; *ABOVE*: ILLUSTRATION SHOWING LAKE AND ENTRANCE FRONTS; *BELOW*: VIEW OF LAKE AND ENTRANCE FRONTS

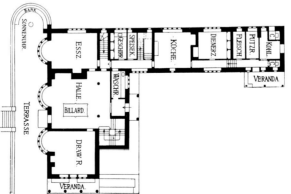

*OPPOSITE*: VIEW FROM THE LAKE; *ABOVE*: MAIN HALL; *BELOW*: GROUND-FLOOR PLAN; *OVERLEAF*: VIEW OF LAKE FRONT

*ABOVE*: VIEW OF ENTRANCE FRONT; *BELOW*: DRAWING ROOM

*ABOVE*: CLOSE-UP OF LAKE FRONT; *BELOW*: DINING ROOM; *OVERLEAF*: VIEW OF ENTRANCE FRONT AND COURTYARD

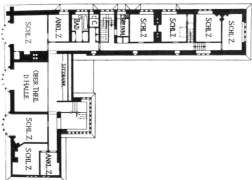

*OPPOSITE*: VIEW OF ENTRANCE FRONT; *ABOVE*: STAIRWAY; *BELOW*: FIRST-FLOOR PLAN

# MOORCRAG, 1898
## *LAKE WINDERMERE, CUMBRIA*

Designed in 1898 for JW Buckley, the house has recently been sympathetically divided into two units.

Moorcrag is less formal than its neighbour, Broadleys, which Voysey built in the same year. This may well be a reflection of the relative difference in status between the two patrons. As a colliery owner, Currer Briggs must have had a considerable sense of self importance. Moorcrag's impact, however, has not been in the least diminished by the ravages of shifting aesthetic standards. It remains a serene and delightful house.

*OPPOSITE*: SIDE VIEW FROM THE NEWLY CONSTRUCTED DRIVEWAY; *ABOVE*: ILLUSTRATION SHOWING THE HOUSE AS ONE UNIT;
*BELOW*: VIEW OF ENTRANCE FRONT; *OVERLEAF*: VIEW FROM THE GARDEN

*OPPOSITE*: VIEW SHOWING DIVISION OF GARDEN FRONT; *ABOVE*: CLOSE-UP OF GARDEN FRONT; *BELOW*: VIEW OF MAIN FACADE; *OVERLEAF*: SIDE ELEVATION

*OPPOSITE*: VIEW SHOWING CHIMNEY; *ABOVE AND BELOW*: GROUND-FLOOR HALL AND SCULLERY; *OVERLEAF*: VIEW OF GARDEN FRONT

*OPPOSITE*: VIEW OF GARDEN FRONT FEATURING LEFT GABLE; *ABOVE*: FIRST-FLOOR BEDROOM; *BELOW*: GROUND-FLOOR SCULLERY

ABOVE: ILLUSTRATIONS OF FRONT AND REAR ELEVATIONS INCLUDING BASEMENT AND GROUND-FLOOR PLANS

# SPADE HOUSE, 1899
## *FOLKESTONE, KENT*

*The house was designed for HG Wells. Although important because of this connection – Wells wrote some of his most famous works here – it does not show Voysey at his best. The original designs went through considerable changes, probably due to limited funds.*

*Spade House acquired its name when Wells resisted having Voysey's favourite heart shape on the front door. Voysey simply added a stalk to the heart, turned it upside down, and transformed it into a symbol of spring, the spade.*

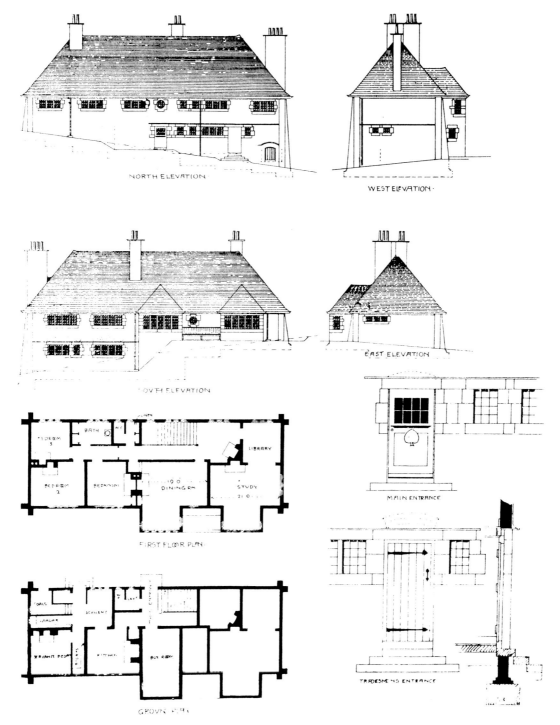

FROM ABOVE: NORTH AND WEST ELEVATIONS; SOUTH AND EAST ELEVATIONS; FIRST-FLOOR PLAN AND MAIN ENTRANCE; GROUND-FLOOR PLAN AND TRADESMEN'S ENTRANCE

*ABOVE*: GARDEN FRONT; *BELOW*: LIVING-ROOM

# THE ORCHARD, 1899
## *CHORLEY WOOD, BUCKINGHAMSHIRE*

*Situated within easy commuting distance of his London office, this house was built by Voysey for his family. Probably for this reason the exterior of The Orchard was far more modest than the architect's usual commissions. Widely publicised, however, it was frequently – though not always successfully – imitated.*

*Woodwork in the house was painted in white enamel,*

*with the exception of the well-known staircase which was of unstained oak. The curtains were bright Turkey red. The entire bedroom floor was covered in green cork carpet tiles. Voysey, though an excellent designer of wallpapers, tended not to include them in the interiors of his clients' houses. However, he used some of them here in his own home, where colour abounded.*

*ABOVE: HALL; BELOW: BEDROOM*

*ABOVE*: VIEW OF GARDEN FRONT; *BELOW*: CLOSE-UP OF GARDEN FRONT SHOWING DOOR

# VODIN, 1902
## *PYRFORD COMMON, SURREY*

*Although lacking the distinction of Greyfriars, Broadleys or Moorcrag, this is an admirable example of Voysey's mature style. Untypically, the roof is clad with tiles, rather than the grey-green slates which Voysey normally favoured. Angled buttresses, strengthening a projecting bay, give Vodin a superficially medievalising appearance. As on so many occasions this reminds us that Voysey never entirely rejected the Gothic Revival influences which he had absorbed as a young man in JP Seddon's office.*

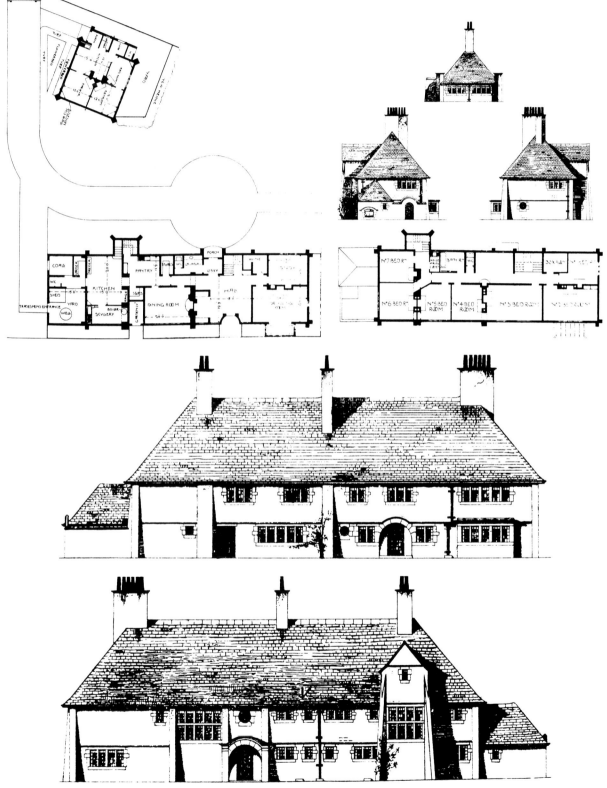

*ABOVE*: GROUND-FLOOR PLAN OF HOUSE AND COTTAGE; COTTAGE ELEVATION WITH WEST AND EAST ELEVATIONS OF HOUSE; PLAN OF BEDROOMS; *MIDDLE AND BELOW*: SOUTH AND NORTH ELEVATIONS OF HOUSE

*ABOVE*: VIEW OF COURTYARD; *BELOW*: VIEW OF GARDEN FRONT AND COURTYARD

# THE PASTURES, 1901

## *NORTH LUFFENHAM, LEICESTERSHIRE*

*Voysey wanted the house to have exposed stone walls, but his client, Miss G Conant, insisted on them being roughcast. (A fellow Arts and Crafts architect, Ernest Gimson, had designed a stone cottage in Leicestershire of which Voysey was very likely aware.)*

*In the interior, the hall and offices were paved with slabs of local stone. All the tiled fireplaces had individual designs by C Dressler of Marlow. The walls of the parlour were hung with pink silk below the frieze; the floors were covered with wall-to-wall self-coloured Austrian-pile carpets.*

*One is reminded by The Pastures of the well-known passage from* News from Nowhere, *1890, in which William Morris dreams of the buildings of the 21st century: 'handsome and generously solid . . . countryfied . . . like yeomen's dwellings'.*

*ABOVE AND BELOW:* VIEW AND DRAWING OF GARDEN FRONT

# WHITE HORSE INN, 1905
## *STETCHWORTH, CAMBRIDGESHIRE*

This was commissioned by the Earl of Ellesmere. The Earl, however, remained not entirely satisfied with the design until it had been reworked several times. Voysey produced a design which represents an updating of the traditional village inn. The almost puritanical simplicity and rustic vocabulary of the White Horse Inn contrasts with the vulgar ornateness of the typical Edwardian public house.

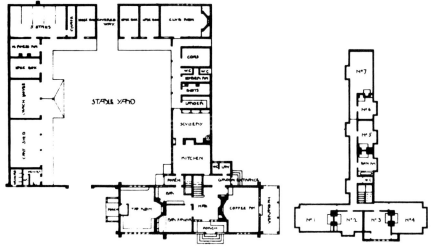

*ABOVE*: FRONT VIEW OF INN; *MIDDLE*: ILLUSTRATION OF INN WITH STABLE; *BELOW*: GROUND-FLOOR PLAN OF INN WITH STABLE AND FIRST-FLOOR PLAN OF INN

# HOLLYMOUNT, 1905
## *KNOTTY GREEN, BUCKINGHAMSHIRE*

*Commissioned by CT Burke, this house presented itself as a rare opportunity for Voysey to design everything from exterior to interior details.*

*Hollymount is modest in its vocabulary. Roughcast, it has a rectangular plan with gables at either end. The roofs are a green slate and the plinths are tarred. Tarred plinths are a vernacular feature which Voysey had started introducing into his work in c1900.*

*ABOVE*: VIEW FROM THE ROAD; *BELOW*: DRAWING OF VIEW FROM THE ROAD

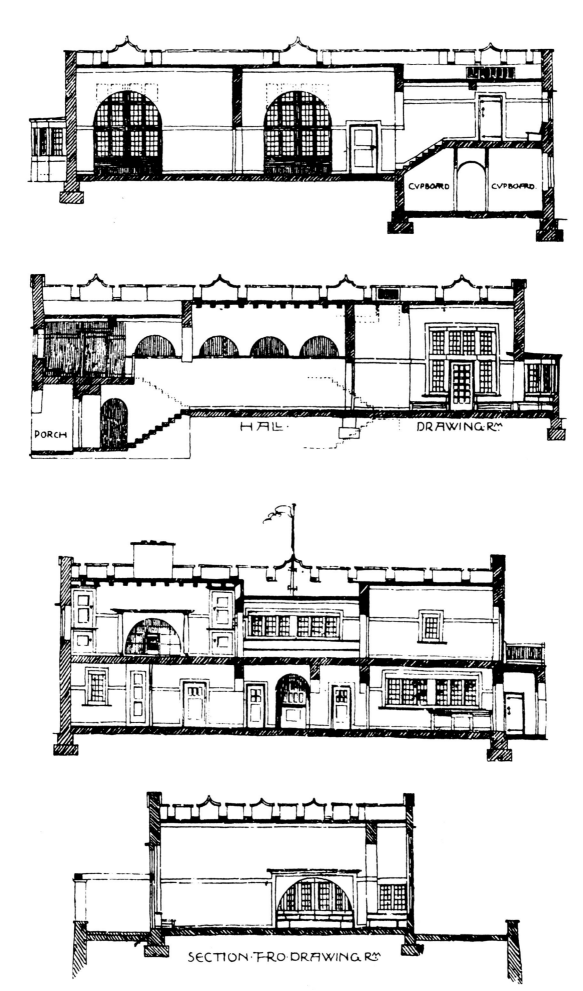

FROM ABOVE: LONG SECTIONS THROUGH DRAWING-ROOM AND THROUGH HALL, CROSS SECTIONS THROUGH DINING-ROOM AND THROUGH DRAWING-ROOM

# HOUSE IN ASWAN, 1905

## *EGYPT*

*Designed and built for Dr HE Leigh Canney, the house probably no longer exists. It remains a mystery as to how Voysey acquired this unusual commission.*

*The preliminary and final designs for the house vary only slightly, and show a more or less rectangular plan. Voysey's customary roughcast walls and stone-dressed windows were used, but concessions to the climate comprised airy living rooms one and a half storeys high, verandahs and balconies, and a flat roof, which was given a castellated outline edged with red tile coping. On two sides the house was raised on a stone-walled platform which extended as terraces.*

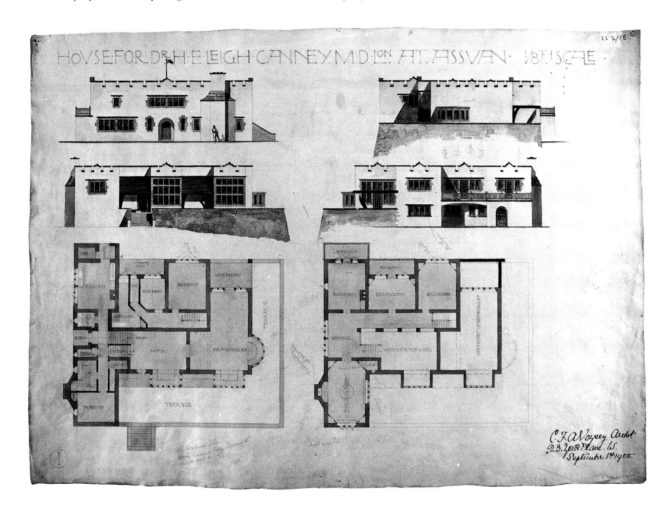

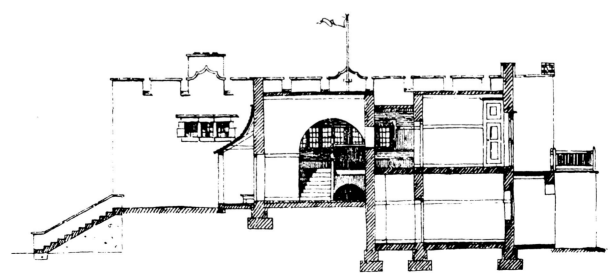

*ABOVE*: SIDE, FRONT AND REAR ELEVATIONS; GROUND-FLOOR AND FIRST-FLOOR PLANS; *BELOW*: CROSS SECTION THROUGH HALL

*ABOVE*: SOUTH-EAST VIEW OF HOUSE; *BELOW*: MAIN FACADE

# THE HOMESTEAD, 1905
## *FRINTON-ON-SEA, ESSEX*

A seaside home built for SC Turner. A bachelor, Turner gave Voysey a free hand as far as the arrangement of the interior and the furnishings were concerned.

Characteristically roughcast with a hipped roof, the house is L-shaped and medium sized. The main feature of the ground floor is a large billiard-cum-sitting room which serves well as an all-purpose room. Inside, the house has exposed beams with plain whitewashed walls and a white tiled ingle-nook with a flat arch top; the quarry tile floor was only partially carpeted.

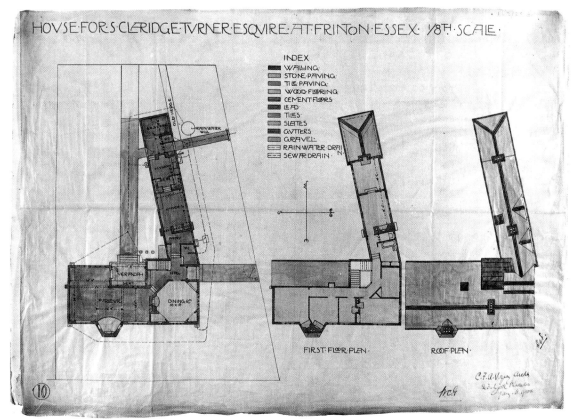

*ABOVE*: VIEW FROM GARDEN; *BELOW*: GROUND-FLOOR, FIRST-FLOOR AND ROOF PLANS

*ABOVE*: HALLWAY; *BELOW*: VIEW FROM THE ROAD

*ABOVE*: BILLIARD-CUM-SITTING ROOM; *BELOW*: GARDEN VIEW SHOWING VERANDAH

*ABOVE*: GARDEN FRONT; *BELOW*: REAR VIEW

# LITTLEHOLME, 1906-07
## *GUILDFORD, SURREY*

*This house was designed for George Muntzer, a successful builder who had worked on some of Voysey's Surrey houses. Littleholme – it is probable that the name was suggested by Voysey himself – was situated on the side of a steep south-facing hill. Voysey was always at his best with challenging and spectacular sites as he was with his two finest houses, Greyfriars (1897) and Broadleys (1898). Though less assertive than in these two earlier works, Littleholme is to be numbered among Voysey's more successful country houses. It lacks, however, the leitmotifs in which Voysey delighted such as the sweeping roofs of Greyfriars or the bays of Broadleys.*

*ABOVE:* GARDEN FRONT SHOWING ENTRANCE; *BELOW:* DRAWING OF GARDEN FRONT

*ABOVE*: VIEW FROM GARDEN

# LITTLEHOLME, 1909
## *KENDAL, CUMBRIA*

*Designed for a furniture maker, AW Simpson, Littleholme was built entirely of local stone by Kendal craftsmen. Although much more modest in scale and design than Greyfriars, or neighbouring Broadleys, or Moorcrag,* *Littleholme makes a surprisingly powerful statement. Voysey was evidently at his best when working with a sympathetic client. Simpson, who worked in the Arts and Crafts tradition, clearly shared Voysey's ideals.*

*ABOVE*: LIVING-ROOM; *BELOW*: EXTERIOR VIEW SHOWING PORCH

# LODGE STYLE, 1909
## *COMBE DOWN, NEAR BATH*

This commission was awarded by TS Cotterell, a quarry owner, who wanted a house reminiscent of Merton College, Oxford, built from his own stone.

The house is entirely Gothic Revival in spirit, providing further evidence of Voysey's attachment to the ideals of JP Seddon. Planned around a 40 by 30 feet quadrangle, the plan was whittled down in scale – for reasons of cost – so that it was 23 by 21 feet. In stylistic terms, Lodge Style could almost pass for a parish school of the 1840s.

*OPPOSITE*: VIEW FROM GARDEN; *ABOVE*: VIEW OF EXTERIOR SHOWING BOTH WINGS; *BELOW*: INTERIOR

HEAD OF STAIRCASE AT GARDEN CORNER, LONDON, c1908

# AN INTERVIEW WITH CFA VOYSEY, ARCHITECT AND DESIGNER
## *THE STUDIO*

So far as it concerns the general public, it is curious to note how the mere accident of his material determines the popular recognition of an artist. Oil paintings and pictures generally are signed, books and musical compositions are also inseparably associated with their authors; but architectural works, and the whole mass of decorative designs, whether in carving, furniture, wallpapers, or the thousand and one applied arts, are entirely anonymous to the majority of people. True, a very important edifice is vaguely assigned to one architect, who is supposed to be responsible for everything connected with it; yet even such partial recognition is so limited that it only serves to emphasise the general neglect of the individual designer. Possibly this is not an unmixed evil. At a meeting of the Japan Society lately, a young Japanese pointed out that where Japan was most artistic it was almost unconscious of the fact, and that then the work itself attracted more attention than its maker. 'Here,' he said, 'if you want a new coinage your RAs design it – it is illustrated in the papers, and generally talked about; in Japan, even today, when we have a new coin, we look at it and see it is beautiful, but do not ask who made it.' If therefore we need not censure the habit of judging most decorative work on its own merits, rather than as a factor in the making of its creator's fame, yet to those technically concerned with the arts, the personality and opinions of a designer should be at least as interesting as those of a picture painter. Today interviewers have left little mystery connected with the professional life of our painters, and we know their appearances, their studios, their views (and their prejudices in many cases), as well as we know their works; indeed, in not a few cases it would be easy to find a person well equipped on all the anecdotal sides of modern art, who has at the same time no power of identifying unsigned work by its own characteristic qualities...

The first thing notable in the old-fashioned little house that is situated in one of the pleasant bye-roads of St John's Wood, was that it appeared exactly the right place for the abode of a creator of beautiful patterns. Screened from the road, with its windows opening on a tree-bordered lawn, for all one saw or heard of the mighty city it might have been in the corner of a cathedral close. Within, passing directly to the studio, one saw it was obviously not merely a work place but a living place, the reticence of its decoration, its furniture bearing the unmistakable impress of the owner's hand, showing that the creed of the artist was the creed he lived. One of the most beautiful of his possessions – a rosy-faced, flaxenhaired lad of four, clad in a blue smock – seemed the very spirit of design in its native simplicity, and as a mere scheme of colour a thing not beaten by any of the charming patterns Mr Voysey unspread at my request. To be quite fair to a very patient host, it must be explained that the following interview, although mainly the artist's replies to my leading questions, includes quotations from a paper read to a meeting of art-workers.

As wallpapers represent a large bulk of Mr Voysey's designs for commerce, it was natural to ask him for his idea of a good design for this material, which despite all attack seems still the clothing of most rooms. To this question Mr Voysey replied, that in his opinion 'a wallpaper should be always essentially a pattern, the repeat of which is recognised as one of its chief characteristics, rather than a pattern disguising the repeat and presenting in detail interwoven pretty bits known to the trade as 'all-over patterns'. 'In other words, you would have the limitations recognised exactly as when in stained glass an artist makes the lead lines a prominent feature, instead of trying to ignore their presence?'

Yes, I think that a wallpaper, even if more pleasing in an all over pattern, is less disturbing when a more determined and simple expression of one or two ideas, unless of course you are one of those unhappy mortals who never notice a design except to count its repetition. A wallpaper is of course only a background, and were your furniture good in form and colour a very simple or quite undecorated treatment of the walls would be preferable; but as most modern furniture is vulgar or bad in every way, elaborate papers of many colours help to disguise its ugliness. Although elaboration makes confusion more confounded, yet if you have but enough confusion the ugliness of modern life becomes bearable. Mr Morris is credited with the axiom 'the smaller your room the larger the pattern you may put on your walls'. There is no doubt that it is better to have large and bold than small and timid patterns, both in papers and printed or stencilled friezes. If you wish to reduce the effect of its scale and force, these can be modified in the colouring. Do not think that I place wallpapers first. Wooden panelling, whether polished or hand-stained, is best of all; next to that comes painted panelling, but as papers wear better than the plain wall, we must permit them to exist on this ground. If, however, the room be a well-proportioned one and the furniture good, even if pictures are absent, the need for wallpapers is not apparent on aesthetic grounds; but in such a case the frieze may be treated with a pattern either printed or stencilled, not too engrossing, but yet sufficiently important...

'You do not consider the ornament on a paper should be limited to strictly conventional foliage and purely ornamental motives?'

No, I do not see why the forms of birds, for instance, may not be used, provided they are reduced to mere symbols. Decorators complain of small repeats and simple patterns, because they are apt to show the joints, and because the figures may be mutilated, in turning a corner for instance. If the form be sufficiently conventionalised the mutilation is not felt; a real bird with his head cut off is an unpleasant sight, so is a rose that has lost half an inch of its petals; but if the bird is a crude symbol and his facsimile occurs complete within ten and a half inches' distance, although one may have lost a portion of his body, it does not violate my feelings. To go to Nature is, of course, to approach the fountain-head, but a literal transcript will not result in good ornament; before a living plant a man must go through an elaborate process of selection and analysis, and think of the balance, repetition, and many other qualities of his design, thereby calling his individual taste into play and adding a human interest to his work. If he does this, although he has gone directly to Nature, his work will not resemble any of his predecessors; he has become an inventor. The ordinary practice is to paraphrase a popular design, one that has sold well. 'We want something in this style,' the manufacturers cry; so, instead of inventing a new

*ABOVE*: ORIGINAL HAND-PAINTED DESIGN, 1913; *FACING PAGE*: DESIGN FOR A WALLPAPER, WATERSNAKES AMONGST WEED, c1889

TULIP TEXTILE DESIGN

pattern, the artist translates an already popular one, and re-adapts its essential qualities in a more or less novel fashion.

It seems to me that to produce satisfactory works, we must acquire a complete knowledge of our material, and be thorough masters of the craft to be employed in its production. Then, working always reasonably, with a sense of fitness, the result will be at least healthy, natural, and vital; even if it be ugly and unpleasing, it will yet give some hope. The danger today lies in over decoration; we lack simplicity and have forgotten repose, and so the relative value of beautiful things is confounded. In most modern drawing-rooms confusion is the first thing that strikes one. Nowhere is there breadth, dignity, repose, or true richness of effect, but a symbolism of money alone. Hoarding pretty things together is more often a sign of vanity and vainglory than good taste.

Instead of painting boughs of apple-trees on our door panels and covering every shelf with petticoats of silk, let us begin by discarding the mass of useless ornaments and banishing the millinery that degrades our furniture and fittings. Reduce the variety of patterns and colours in a room. Eschew all imitations, and have each thing the best of its sort, so that the decorative value of each will stand forth with increased power and charm, and concentrated richness will be more apparent with its simple neighbours.

To produce healthy art one must have healthy surroundings; the first effort an artist should make is to sweep ugliness away from himself.

The habit of being merely tenants, on short leases, of our homes has fostered the vice which crowds foolish and useless objects, bad in proportion and colour, into rooms ugly and uncomfortable in themselves. We pitch ornamentation in our rooms with no restraint. We have a language of ornament and yet nothing to say – charmed by its sound, we have let vanity feed on its own creations, and forgotten that the expression of deep and noble feelings would make decorative art once again full of life and vigour.

It is not necessary for artists to be bound merely to tradition and precedent, or to be crammed to overflowing with the knowledge of the products of foreign nations. They should each use their God-given faculties, and if they have thoughts worth expressing, the means to express them sufficiently are, and always will be, at hand. Not that we need shut our eyes to all human efforts, but we should go to Nature direct for inspiration and guidance. Then we are at once relieved from restrictions of style or period, and can live and work in the present with laws revealing always fresh possibilities.

Then Mr Voysey showed me a portfolio of designs. . . The well-known 'Troillus' paper made by Messrs Essex, the 'Buttercups and Daisies', and a host of good patterns to be seen in the best shops, bear witness to the variety and fertility of his invention. These, however, with the introduction of animal life and their boldly presented repeats are typical instances of his individual taste.

Some of the designs owe so much to their colour that it is necessary to convey some hint of their scheme to explain the black and white reductions. In one frieze the bright-yellow green of the chestnut-trees is in perfect balance with the pale green of the upper row of tree-tops, the flights of sky-blue birds above, and the crouching figures in greys and blues below. The band of dark colour so noticeable in the reproduction is not felt in the gay yet soft colour of the original. In the design of 'Birds and Berries', the deep yellow of the birds, perched on pale green stalks among berries of salmon and creamy yellow, is balanced by the blue-green of the conventional leaf form, and the harmony kept without the least sense of 'spottiness' which the black and white facsimile undoubtedly has. In the 'Seven Sisters', the dull Venetian blue of the sea throws up the stems, trunks, and sails, which are an orange red, the hills being alternately brown and sage green. In 'The Demon', a daring harmony in reds and yellows like a Gaillardia blossom is heightened by the cunning touches of dark green in the background, hardly noticeable without close study. The 'Sea-gulls' is much distorted, in the original the birds are a neutral grey-blue and in the same tone as the two blues of the conventional sea, their yellow-green bills being bright notes of colour. The most sumptuous 'Three Men of Gotham', recalls stained glass in its lustrous harmony: the sea is peacock green, the boats olive and sage green, the sails red and orange, the men a duller red, with the lightest touches in the yellow-green pennants, and white sea-birds like flashes of actual light in the sky between; it is not possible in words to convey the richness of the broken colour.

Among the most striking instances of Mr Voysey's power to take a commonplace subject and impart to it distinct individuality, a design for a cottage piano, may be specially mentioned. In this the shafts which support the key-board rise on either side to the height of the instrument, with arrangements to hold candles, are the most prominent features, and give an architectural dignity to the otherwise commonplace piece of furniture, without in any way detracting from its utility, but, on the contrary, adding features for common everyday use. It is only just to the author of a very charmingly designed piano, made by Messrs Bechstein, to note here that he worked out the same problem on not dissimilar lines, but the coincidence is purely fortuitous, neither artist having known the scheme of the other. This regard for utility, which is the basis of beauty, is apparent also in the design for the kettle stand in wrought metal we reproduce, which is both comely and substantial.

It is not fair to regard Mr Voysey as a designer alone. An architect by profession, his chief occupation is still concerned with the building itself, and a design for a cottage for an artist, no less than a mansion, staircase for instance show that fertility of invention and a curiously individual quality, at once simple and noble, are as apparent in his architectural as in his graphic work.

One of the charms of his objects is their domesticity – gorgeous enough for palaces, you would not find they rendered a twenty-pound house mean by their intrusion; on the contrary, they beautify all they come in contact with, unless placed next to vicious and vulgar ornamentation; but even then it is not Mr Voysey's work that suffers. To be simple is the end, not the beginning, of design; complexity hides a multitude of shortcomings, simplicity shows boldly its faults no less than its virtues. The simplicity which is the highest effort is the selection of essential beauty from all possible ornament, reduced to its most direct expression. Like the poetry of the phrase 'green pastures by still waters', you feel nothing can be added to the perfection of the description; and so in much of Mr Voysey's work the flat tints and almost child-like rendering of the chosen forms are the result of the same employment of the right word, the right form, the right colour – without apparent effort – which if not high art, as people misunderstand it, is at least beauty, and a distinct effort to work as Nature herself works.

Before leaving, my host took me through his house, and although it would be out of place to speak of the various pieces of furniture, the clever adaptation of use to beauty, one could not but feel that here was proof of comfort and domestic requirements combined with art in a way that made it remarkable. Stepping from its ordered simplicity into the streets, the first upholsterer's window pointed the moral still more plainly, and made one realise, despite the efforts of William Morris, of art-workers, writers, and lecturers, how wide a gulf still yawns between the furnishing of the house today as it might be, and the newly revived horrors of the Rococo, the superfluities, the cheap bric-a-brac and the costly – which are all more or less rubbish; and yet, ephemeral though they may be, usurp the majority of houses today.

*Extracts taken from* The Studio, *I, 1893, pp232-37.*

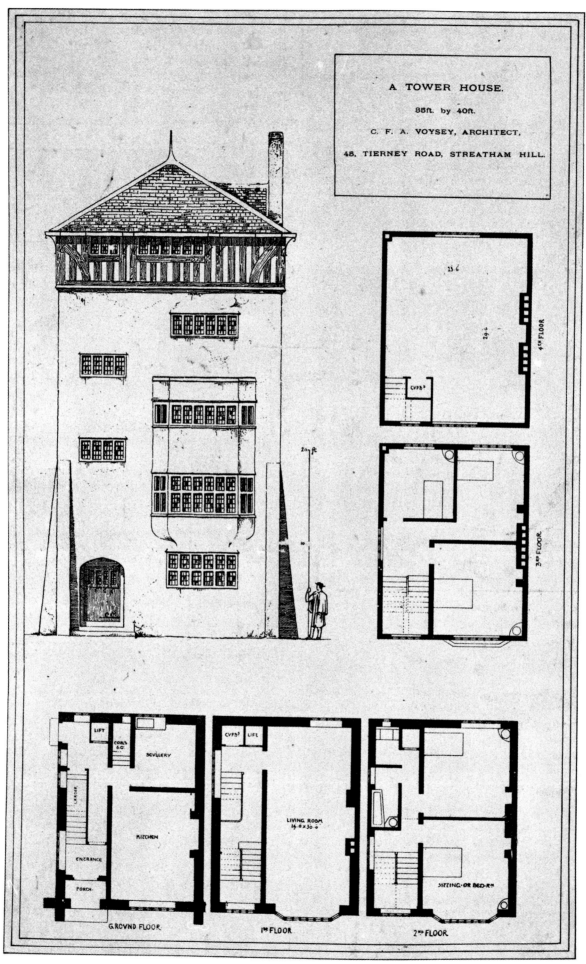

UNEXECUTED DESIGN FOR A TOWER HOUSE, 1889

# THE REVIVAL OF ENGLISH DOMESTIC ARCHITECTURE

## *THE STUDIO*

The former chapters [in *The Studio*, June 1897] on the revival of English domestic architecture have been devoted to the work of men long since recognised as masters, and have embraced palaces and mansions as well as houses for people of moderate incomes. But the work of Mr CFA Voysey to be considered here belongs to quite another order. For it is no exaggeration to say that some of the entirely delightful houses he has called into being would compare favourably in cost with the miserable shams of the jerry-builder. To beat the vulgar and badly constructed dwelling – on economic as well as artistic grounds – is a notable achievement. But that Mr Voysey has done it more than once remains as abiding evidence that art may not only be obedient to the demands of common sense, but that it is able to use worthy materials honestly, and give you a lasting structure as cheaply as the most scamping rival could produce it. This is doubtless due to the fact that Mr Voysey in such a building almost entirely ignores ornament, especially of the sort that is applied so lavishly to distract attention from faulty workmanship and unsound material.

It is often the plaint of poor but artistic house-builders, that lack of money obliges them to forego beautiful things. This is a fallacy of the worst order. For it implies that beauty is a thing of decoration and non-essentials. In theory we all agree to protest against such a distorted view of beauty; but in practice, especially in architectural practice, the presence of so much superfluous, if not, possibly, bad ornament, can be attributed to no other cause. But because Mr Voysey in almost every case hitherto, has abjured carvings, stained glass, tiles, and the ordinary items of applied decoration, it would be absurd to argue there from his dislike or contempt. Should he ever accept a commission to build a palace for a millionaire (and one may be sure he would not unless he had full liberty to discard the commonplace decorations of the hour) then we have no reason to suppose it would be unadorned. On the contrary while we should find exquisite proportion and harmonious arrangement of masses his first aims, there is little doubt, but that he would employ fellow craftsmen to enrich certain portions as superbly as they knew how. One sees in his furniture no reliance on mouldings or machine carvings, ormolu mountings, or other 'stuck on' decorations; but all the same in hinges, escutcheons, and other portions where ornament can be used wisely, he does not shun it, but rather welcomes and amplifies it so that these few portions impart the effect of sumptuous adornment to the whole of a structure that else relies solely on good material, shaped to fine proportion.

In another context he has explained his theory of the decoration of the house. If you have beautiful furniture, and fine pictures, and such pieces of bric-a-brac as are entitled to be called works of art, then he counsels exquisite reticence in internal decoration. But if you must needs use unlovely ornate furniture, and fabrics with patterns, then he would have you unafraid to welcome pattern everywhere; so that in its very abundance you may escape the contours of badly shaped furniture sharply defined against a plain wall, or some one dominant pattern thrusting itself on you without any rivals to modify its insistent claim to be noticed.

That Mr Voysey is fond of green-painted woodwork, or of green-coloured furniture, one has heard urged against him. This is as ignoble a reason for urging against a craftsman's schemes as the ordinary slang of the 'art-at-home' columns of weekly papers. There, we read lately, 'green furniture is coming in again,' as if it were a mode in hair-dressing, or a fabric for spring costumes. If with experience of its utility, and with full belief in its economy, you find a certain treatment for woodwork, structural or movable, better adapted than others, why for the sake of variety should you use less admirable methods?

Painting in simple, pleasant colours has found its opponents at certain times. Yet the common-stained deal of the mission-room Gothic, or the small vicarage, is no more honest. It is more indiscreet, but indiscretion is not necessarily truth. Mr Voysey's doctrine of honesty is not founded on quibbles of this sort. Paint will not hide bad material, and cover up clumsy workmanship from the eye of an expert. But well applied it can give a far more pleasant surface than is likely to be obtained from cheap wood, smeared with a sticky-looking varnish.

There is such a thing as sham honesty, an affectation of being superior to one's fellows in exact truth of statement, which is not far removed from hypocrisy, although it aims to be at the very opposite extreme. As, for example, in woodwork of the Early Victorian Gothic revival, where every mortice showed its keyed tenon, and buttresses, whether needed or not by the construction was a favourite motive in buildings as well as furniture. In Mr Voysey's designs for small houses buttresses frequently occur, but these are not used because mediaeval builders employed them, still less are they added to walls already strong enough to impart a 'quaint' or 'picturesque' effect. Mr Voysey employs these buttresses to save the cost of thicker walls for the lower storey of his buildings. That they chance to afford pleasant-looking shelters for a garden seat, and break up the wall-surface happily, giving the facade a certain architectural pattern of shadows he realises, and is, beyond doubt, delighted by the picturesque qualities which happen to result from their use. Although the fact is patent enough from study of the architect's works, it may be as well to re-state it – Mr Voysey would no more dream of adding a superfluous buttress than he would add an unnecessary panel of cheap ornament. If, after knowledge of his designs, you still believe he is purposely eccentric, or deliberately strains after unusual effects, it does but prove how hard it is for any sincere worker to express himself that all who run may read clearly, and that those not sympathetic can realise his intentions.

Unless one approaches Mr Voysey's designs for houses with some appreciation of his intention, there is danger in confusing his essential principles with those which chance to be also aesthetic. No one who sketches from Nature will deny that a Voysey cottage is a far more seemly building for the foreground of a fine landscape than is the average suburban villa with 'high art', as commerce understands it, proclaimed boldly, in every detail. Given a few creeping plants, and some time-stains – that last painting which nature slowly but gratuitously adds to every picture, and the houses he has built fall into the scheme of an English landscape as harmoniously as do the thatched cottages of a past century. That this quality of accord with nature is rare in modern architecture needs no examples adduced for proof. A view from any railway-carriage window will discover a thousand discordant objects of the

*ABOVE*: NORNEY, 1897; *BELOW*: HOLLYMOUNT, 1905

country. Without quoting any instances in our own land, who can forget the perky little French villas which do so much to vulgarise the exquisite apple-orchards of Normandy in the spring, when after a mile of pure Corot, or Harpignies, the eye is arrested by a little toy 'maisonette', which in its trim angularity strikes a discordant note at once, as if you perched the latest thing in Paris hats on one of the seated Graces of the Parthenon.

Were the good qualities of Mr Voysey's building all told in this statement, and their one claim to artistic approval rested on their relation to the landscape around, enough would be proved to warrant his claim to a very honourable place among modern architects. For of only a very few could as much be said truly – and one doubts where in any other case such economy of money or material could also be claimed for the same works.

But there is another side – and a very important one it is. If you study the plans of his small houses, you will be amazed to find how liberal is the space compared with the cost of the building. You will also discover that he believes in the importance of one or two large rooms – large, that is to say, in proportion to the dimensions of the whole building – instead of a lot of little rooms and narrow, unnecessary passages.

Readers of *The Studio* will possibly remember a plan and elevation for an artist's cottage (Vol IV 34), where in a building estimated to cost between £700 and £800 there was a living-room 28 ft by 14 ft. This of course was in place of two so-called drawing and dining-rooms, 14 ft by 14 ft, which the average little villa would offer you; but although there was no other 'reception-room', a passage at the back was widened, and by the addition of a bay window figured as a smoking-room, or picture-gallery, some 20 ft long, by 9 ft wide in the bay and 6 ft at either end. In short, the house was planned for people who prefer the easy, if unconventional *ménage*, to the discomfort of the dull, orthodox routine. In place of a stuffy little parlour, and an equally stuffy little feeding apartment, you had one spacious room and one handy lounge, available when domestic economy required the other to be given up to 'laying the cloth' or other household duties.

It is perhaps this tendency of real economy designed to provide for actual comfort in place of imaginary luxury which repels certain people from Mr Voysey's work. In the last *Arts and Crafts* a roofed bedroom chair was the object of much zealous detraction. As it chanced, the present writer when writing about this particular item was undergoing the ordinary discomfort of a common cold, and sitting at his work beneath a studio sky-light; consequently he thought of the chair with personal recognition of its draught-screening powers, and wished he had been lucky enough to own it. He did not think of it as one of eight or ten – all hooded – around a dining-room table, because it was clearly intended for an invalid's use. Yet to hear certain comments upon it, one would have supposed that it was Mr Voysey's idea of a work-a-day chair, subject to many changes of place. So the cottages he plans for ample sites, with side as well as front lighting, must not be criticised as his idea of a small house in a London street. You have but to study certain houses in Hans Place, SW3, to see that the architect is quite as able to grapple with the artificial conditions of crowded life in a neighbourhood where ground is costly, as with a cottage site where land is cheap. Nor if your habit of living necessitates formal hospitality would he give you a living-room and a lounge in place of the conventional reception-rooms of a town mansion. His simplicity of detail may be governed by pecuniary economy in one case; but as you remember the Hans Place houses, you will not find more liberal expenditure lavished upon the ornamental fittings of the builder's catalogue. In England, where domestic life gathers to itself so many purely ornamental objects – pictures, porcelain, and the rest – the rooms themselves cannot fitly receive the same richness of treatment that in a continental salon, with its sparse furniture, seems so eminently

right. Here the two styles are not pitted against each other, for both are legitimate provision for the actual needs of the occupant. But recognising the fondness of an English householder for all sorts of extraneous objects of art and *vertu*, it is well not to make the rooms so completely self-sufficient that every added item helps to mar their original effect.

How well Mr Voysey has realised golden silence and silver speech his designs will show. For if silence is the most precious, yet speech is not despicable. Indeed many of us are bi-metallists in this sense. One form of speech is unluckily prohibited in writing of contemporaries, and that is a description of the personality of the artist. It is true that by his works ye shall know him; yet if a hint of their author's real self could be conveyed at the same time, how much fuller and quicker would they be comprehended. Good taste forbids even the hint, and a dozen anecdotes, a score of sayings uttered unguardedly in private conversation must not be repeated here. But without breaking into the privacy of his life in any way, it is only bare justice to record the fact that Mr Voysey's simplicity of manner, his aim to use honest materials in a straightforward way, his occasional touches of humour, such as appear even in his most important works – all these are the open expression of the man as well as of the architect. Some natures are dual, and with no conscious hypocrisy a man holds quite different creeds for his professional duties and his personal habits. We have known people austere and ascetic, who were prodigals and incontinent in their art, also people who preferred rigid simplicity for their own surroundings, and yet delighted in making those of other people gorgeous, if not absolutely vulgar; others with a professed hatred of shams, who were so bewildered by some ingenious expedient to gain a splendid effect by means of imitative substitutes for the more costly material, that all their theories were forgotten. But search through Mr Voysey's work as you may, you will find no attempt to produce any effect by imitative means. One other thing may be put on record – namely, his habit of referring directly to Nature for inspiration, and his indifference to precedent; not in any contemptuous attitude of superiority, but in a real feeling of humility which believes Nature to be the source of all, and so prefers to seek the fountain-head direct. One may misunderstand his rigid suppression of ornament so-called, his avoidance of carving and stained glass, and the pretty trifles which the builder of the modern house delights in. Yet to comprehend his attitude, towards the orthodox enrichments of the house it is well to remember that when pattern is required for textiles, papers, or what not, the same artist who is unflinching in repressing it when he believes it will be superfluous, revels in the beauty of intricate line and complex colour when the occasion justifies it. We have, as I said before, many examples of Mr Voysey's economic work, yet we may be sure that if a palace came from his hands it would be distinguished by the larger beauty which makes a Greek temple memorable rather than by the petty ornamentation that has delighted many excellent people in bygone ages no less than today.

The studio for WEF Britten, West Kensington, occupies a unique position for a town house, as it is in the angle of an L-shaped street, and isolated from its neighbours. With its severe outline and pleasantly painted woodwork it arrests your attention and proclaims its author at a glance. Indeed, when you come across it by accident in the very ordinary street, it is almost startling to realise how wide a gulf separates its design from the average town studio. But the site permitted the building, and the architect took full advantage of the unusual conditions.

The two houses, 14 and 16 Hans Road, Chelsea, do not amaze you by sheer novelty as Mr Britten's studio surprises. Yet as you study their simple but dignified facade, once again you recognise Mr Voysey's handling as surely as if his name were written legibly across it. Even in the small scale on which they are shown here, the exquisite sense of proportion, and the reticent use of even purely

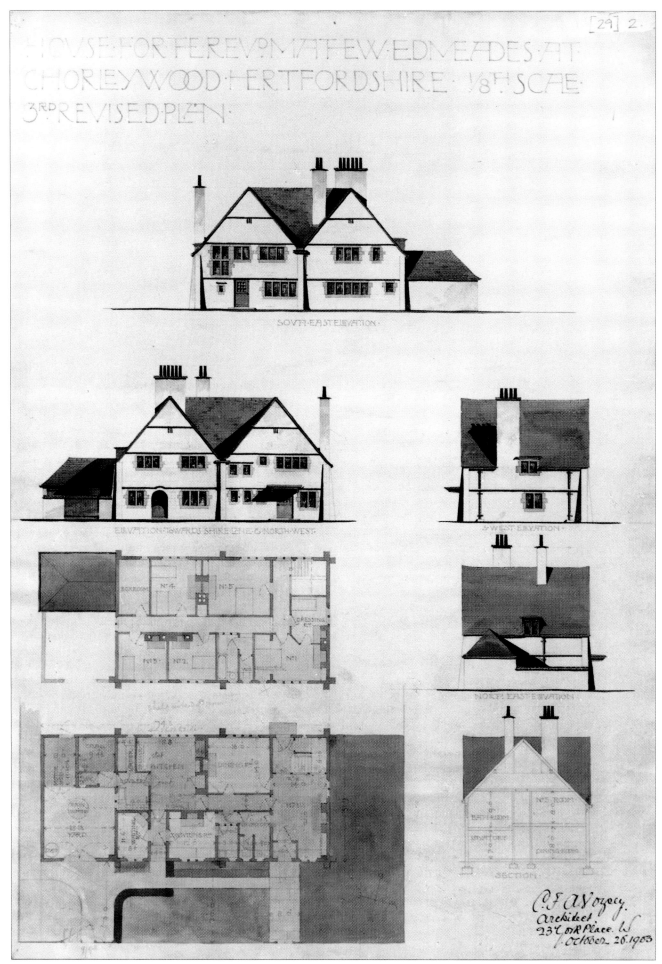

UNEXECUTED DESIGN FOR REV MATTHEW EDMEADES IN CHORLEYWOOD, 1903

architectural features, impress you with a sense of sufficiency. They look what they are, solid, comfortable dwellings, that preserve a distinction all their own even in a neighbourhood where satisfactory houses are not common. It is rare to find personality revealed by simplicity; as a rule it is the flourishes or the eccentricity of the letters which betray handwriting. Here Mr Voysey has no superfluous stroke, no affected detail, and yet his individuality stands clearly revealed.

It is possible that Walnut Tree Farm, would not at once betray its author; but in the second from another point of view there would be little reason for doubt. But the garden front is entirely typical. The four gables breaking the long tiled roof, the buttress to the lower storey, the simple yet novel treatment of the porch, and the placing of the chimney-stacks are entirely characteristic of their author. It is a home worthy of its pastoral name; a building which seems in every way suggestive of the clean, luxurious domesticity of an English homestead; so that as you study it in various photographs and plans you are conscious of a yearning for all the leisurely comforts a visit to such a house implies.

The Six Cottages, in Elmesthorpe, built for the Earl of Lovelace, are particularly picturesque, and they are moreover, extremely commodious and compact. The porches coupled in pairs, with the great eaves of thatch brought over them give a sense of shelter that suggests a hen covering her chickens. The bench outside each porch is the only addition to the bare necessities of a house, and yet this simple and inexpensive item betrays sympathy with the inmates – a reward of rest after honest labour. In touches of this sort Mr Voysey betrays plainly the accord with humanity which softens the apparent austerity of his work. His 'extras' do not take the form of ornament, not even of a decorated inscription setting forth the glory of the architect; but when they are apparent, they are invariably planned to yield some little pleasure to the occupants.

In a House at Frensham, we have a very typical 'Voysey' building. The proportions of the roof, the angle buttresses, the window which breaks into the eaves, the casements, each slightly unlike the other, and especially the curious dormer which appears below the chimney-stack, are distinctly characteristic of Mr Voysey's manner, comely and pleasant. The interior views show the same rigid distrust of ornament. Yet the homely looking, wide fireplace, no less than the more conventional mantelpiece in another room, reveal beauty gained by harmony in the balance of structural parts. In the pillars to the latter mantelpiece Mr Voysey abjures bases for his columns, as he did in another design at the last Arts and Crafts. Whether this innovation is quite justified need not be discussed here, but from long associations there can be little doubt that the absence of a plinth seems a defect. Yet in Egyptian and in Doric architecture this is not felt; but so far as memory serves, the columns in both styles never started from the actual ground level, but from a low wall which is but a plinth of another sort. If only space permitted, it would be interesting to illustrate each facade of this house, which is built in brickwork, cement-roughcast, and lime-washed, roofed with Westmoreland green slates, with lead pipes and ridges. The ideal of a modest country-house is surely realised here. It is not 'a cottage with a double coach-house, a cottage of gentility', Coleridge's delightfully apt instance of the devil's darling sin, 'the pride that apes humility,' but a real cottage that has no pretension and is yet comely enough and commodious enough to be the shooting-box of an emperor.

Perrycroft, Malvern, is a larger building with the L-shaped plan that its author evidently finds peculiarly adapted for domestic requirements. In one arm of the L are the kitchen, scullery, and offices, while the other is devoted to the reception-rooms and bedrooms. As you notice its projecting eaves, its wide windows close beneath, and its massively simple chimney-stacks, it reveals

Mr Voysey's hand, and from the garden, as the two sides are seen, the buttresses which he has made are so peculiarly his own as to dismiss any shadow of suspicion concerning its author.

Perhaps the best known of all this architect's work is An Artist's Cottage at Bedford Park, a white house in the very centre of the red-brick revival, a 'cottage' of three storeys, that contains a studio 31 ft by 17 ft, and a parlour 17 ft 6 in by 14 ft, with three bedrooms and the usual offices. The contract price for this was £494 10s, a price that takes one's breath away, and tempts one to believe that if the site were obtained it would be economic as well as delightful to quit one's present tenancy, and employ Mr Voysey to design another for one's own needs. It is amusing to read that it was found necessary, in order to prevent the builder from displaying the usual 'ovolo mouldings', 'stop chamfers', fillets and the like, to prepare 18 sheets of contract drawings to show where his beloved ornamentation was to be omitted. This topsy-turvy proceeding is delightfully suggestive of the entirely mechanical adornment in general use which is so thoroughly a part of the routine that great pains have to be taken to prevent the workmen from unconscious 'decoration', according to their wonted habit.

There is no doubt that red brick, beautiful as it is in the hands of competent designers, can be vulgarised more easily than simple roughcast lime washed. But the value of Mr Voysey's art is not in the use of any material, or on any mannerism, but in his evident effort to seek first the utilitarian qualities of strength and fitness, and to obtain beauty by common honesty. This separates it at once from the spurious honesty which ultra-Gothic designers made ridiculous; or from an affectation of clumsy simplicity which defeats its purpose.

It is neither Gothic nor Classic architecture which Mr Voysey practises, but house-building pure and simple. The habit of making pretty pictures, to be carried out in all available materials, regardless of cost and, often enough, of good taste also, has not attracted him, as it failed to attract the other men of his profession who have regained a lost position for English domestic architecture.

From the design for a more ambitious work a house for the Earl of Lovelace at Ockham Park, and those drawings which were shown at last year's Academy [1896], the moral to be drawn is somewhat monotonous. But enough has been said to prove that Voysey is not a mere dreamer, but a practical and experienced architect, who will give you first a sanitary, substantial, and comfortable house, and in doing so – with no extra cost – manage to make it a really artistic building at the same time. So rare a combination of fact and fancy deserves reiteration. Hitherto we had imagined that beautiful things – whether Morris cretonnes or Kelmscott Press books – or a hundred less familiar examples, were only to be enjoyed by people of very ample incomes. Voysey does not quote as his motto, 'Economy at any price,' but all the same he gives it you, without sacrificing comeliness and stateliness in so doing. For there is a stateliness of a sort in absence of decoration – as a well known anecdote of an American foreign minister goes to prove. It is not the only way – in certain circumstances it may not even be the best way – but it is a very good plan to take it as a working rule, that all mere ornament is to be viewed with suspicion, and that if even Owen Jones' advice 'decorate your construction, do not construct your decoration' holds a still greater truth – that given the right artist, the construction may be in itself sufficiently beautiful to require no added adornment. Seek first construction, and whether the rest be added unto it or not, the result will be not often unsatisfactory.

*This article appeared in* The Studio, *XI, No 51, June 1897, under the name 'G' – a possible pseudonym for the magazine's editor, Gleeson White.*

# NOTES ON COUNTRY AND SUBURBAN HOUSES

## *HORACE TOWNSEND*

It is not so very many years since it was almost a truism among the architectural profession that the architect who wandered from the strait and narrow path and took to designing furniture, wallpapers, and so forth, had committed a species of professional suicide. Doubtless it was the late EW Godwin[1] who more than any other dissipated this absurd theory, and the 'new architect' nowadays designs the interior, including furniture, hangings, and so forth, of his house, quite as much as he does the exterior. No one in our day, perhaps, has been so completely successful in this respect as Mr CFA Voysey. To introduce Mr Voysey to the readers of *The Studio* were absurd, so familiar are they with what I may almost call, without laying myself open to a charge of exaggeration, his epoch-making work in the decorative field. His furniture, with its broad simple effects, its reliance on proportion, its eschewal of useless ornament, and its strikingly original lines, has helped to form a school of its own, while his wallpapers and textiles strike an equally personal and individual note. Mr Voysey is a designer who is guided, as one need not study him long to perceive, by very definite and certain principles, and, as the accompanying illustrations will serve to show, his architectural work is to just the same extent subservient to these same principles. Simplicity of thought and perfection of proportion distinguish it from the ordinary architecture of the day. Notable, too, is the deliberate avoidance of style; and here it is that only one or two of contemporary architects at the most are working to the same end as Mr Voysey, and endeavouring, by an educated distrust of following too closely on the lines laid down by the craftsmen of the past, to so impress what they do with their own individualities, as to present us with a 19th-century architecture. Whether they be right or wrong, it seems at least certain that by no slavish adherence to tradition has any living, breathing architectural style of bygone centuries come into existence, valuable and necessary as have been the lessons taught by the artists of previous generations.

But let us consider Mr Voysey's work rather more in detail. One's first impression on glancing at the view of the house at North Tooting Common, is of the skill with which so many apparently uncorrelated features have been without effort harmonised and 'pulled together', to use a slang phrase, giving an air of breadth and repose to what might so easily have been an uneasy arrangement of wall space, roof, and window. The plan of this suburban house is also marked by simplicity and ingenuity, one of its leading features being the skill with which the stable has been designed so as to be under the same roof as the rest of the house, and yet be efficiently cut off from the living portion. The best view is to the north, yet Mr Voysey has sensibly placed the chief rooms so as to look south, while the study which Mr Essex chiefly uses during the forenoon catches the rays of the morning sun. The long stretch of reposeful roof is of green slates, the dressings to windows and doors are of Bath stone, while the walls are of roughcast. Mr Voysey's preference for this last-named form of finish – which is marked, by the way – is based, so he tells me, mainly on its economy. He considers a nine-inch brick wall faced with cement roughcast is as warm and weather-tight as any much more expensive construction; but, at the same time, I imagine he is unconsciously attracted by the artistic value of these great spaces of cream-coloured surface,

possessing a texture of their own, and peculiarly lending themselves to Mr Voysey's stylistic sympathies.

Of a totally different character to Mr Essex's house is Broadleys, Windermere, a house built for A Currer Briggs. Here, we have a country house with a dignity all its own, yet based again on the striking simplicity of conception. The hall, that essential feature of a country house, runs up into the roof, with a long glazed gallery at one end. The characteristic windows here were suggested to Mr Voysey by the charming views which the surrounding country affords, while the great bay by which the drawing-room is lighted prevents the interior being in any way darkened by the verandah, which, as shown by the plan, runs along one end of it. From the terrace in front of the house the ground falls down to the lake, affording a delightful prospect of which full advantage is taken by the window arrangement.

Another north-country house is that for WE Rowley, at Glassonby, Kirkoswald, in Cumberland. Here the architect has taken advantage of local material, and in a subtle way, I think, of local feeling. The result is a house which is a study in colour, with its purplish-red sandstone walls, and which also seems, to me, at least, to speak the 'north countree' in its almost puritanical severity. It stands, I am told, on a most beautiful site, overlooking a river and a wild rocky country with which its sturdy uncompromising, straightforwardness seems peculiarly to harmonise. Here again, the bays were considered essential on account of the views, there is a fine entrance hall from which dining-room and drawing-room lead off, while another feature of the plan is the care with which children's and servants' quarters are cut off from the other part of the house.

In Mr Rickard's house at Windermere we have an ideal bachelor's country quarters. The plan is arranged so that all the services of the house can be comfortably carried out, such as access gained to store cupboard, and so on, without infringing on the bachelor's private domain.

The site of this house, also, Mr Voysey characterised as superb, and assures us his chief care was to endeavour to harmonise his house with its surroundings. A fine site, in his estimation, helps to create a beautiful house if the architect is careful not to come into competition with the country surrounding him, but endeavours to subject himself to nature's architecture. It is, I think, this constant subjection to nature as the chief source of inspiration which is one of Mr Voysey's leading characteristics as a decorative designer; and one can see by studying these views of Mr Rickard's house how admirably he has applied the same principle to his architecture. One can imagine how this design, with its mingling of reticence and modest assertion, would appear to be a part of its surroundings. It is this appearance of naturalness, of having grown by degrees rather than having been put there at a single stroke, which is the greatest charm a house in the country can possess, whether it be a simple Surrey cottage or a weather-stained grey stone hall with the traditions of centuries clinging around it. Reverting once more to this Windermere house of Mr Voysey's, it is finished in his favourite roughcast, roofed with green slates, while the chimney-pots which crown the sturdy chimney-stacks are coloured black, no shade of red having by experiment been found to properly harmonise.

Travelling south to the pleasant lanes and well-wooded heights of Sussex and Surrey, we have first Mr Newbold's house at Westmeston, the lower view of which shows us Mr Voysey at his very best. There are few who could have treated the long stretch of unbroken and unrelieved wall space so efficiently, in the relations of wall and window openings, as here appears, while even what one might otherwise feel inclined to stigmatise as the baldness of the porch appears to fit naturally into the scheme. Effective, too, is the garden view of the same wing of the building, with its arched openings – utilitarian, yet strikingly decorative – which give light and air to the tradesmen's entrance corridor. Turning to the plan of this house, we find the staircase well lit by the lantern-light, which offers a picturesque external feature.

I may say in passing that Mr Voysey characterises himself as a 'stickler for light', though, by those who lend a mere surface consideration to his work, he is often found fault with for the smallness of his windows. He points out, however, that such critics do not take into consideration the size and height of the rooms these long low windows are intended to give light to. In proportion to a day; but it is none the less to be regretted that the principles Mr Voysey and a few others have put into such excellent practice as regards the moderate-sized house should not yet, save in one or two instances, have been displayed in regard to buildings of a more monumental character. I do not fail to recognise that in one or two instances London street architecture has been enriched by works which speak directly to us in the 19th-century architectural language. But they are regrettably exceptional. If one can compose, in the architectural language of the 19th century, the dainty lyric overflowing with domestic sentiment, why not the stately ode surcharged with nobility of thought and idea? If, as these examples are, I hope, sufficient to demonstrate, there really is a 19th-century architectural style which is not a mere pastiche of bygone designers' details and fancies, is it not to be regretted that future ages will have to search for it, not in our public buildings, and in the principal streets of our cities, but in the unassuming house or cottage in more or less remote corners of the countryside?

*This extract was taken from* Studio, *XVI, No 73, April 1899.*

**Notes**

1 Edward William Godwin, 1833-86, was the architect of the Aesthetic Movement *par excellence*. He designed the white house for James McNeill Whistler and was a friend of William Burgess. In 1877 he designed a complete range of 'art furniture' – in the 'Anglo Japanese' style – for the manufacturer William Watt. Like Voysey he was an accomplished designer of fabrics and wallpapers.

DRAWING SHOWING DINING ROOM OF THE PASTURES, c1901

VIEW OF VOYSEY'S HOME SHOWING HIS DRAWINGS

# IDEAS IN THINGS

## CFA VOYSEY

I am not here to feel your pulses, diagnose your afflictions, and prescribe any wonderful pill; I have no patent medicine. I believe you are all in excellent health – not bodily health but spiritual health. Yes, you would not be here unless you wanted to improve something, or do some good to somebody, any more than I should, and that is a healthy sign. And, before we part, let us hope we shall all feel that our good desire will ultimately bear good fruit. Let us always carry in our minds the firm conviction that no honest effort is without good fruit. Our accomplishment may be frustrated, but our good intention is always recorded in some way, not necessarily apparent to the world or to ourselves in the way we expect. Neither goodness nor truth can perish. Though we may not see the fruits of our labour, let us believe nothing good is ever wholly lost.

This age we live in is intensely material; it has witnessed a mighty development in material things. Steam and electricity have transformed the world: our minds have been engrossed by material ideas to such an extent that we have scarcely devoted that attention to the spiritual side of our natures which that side deserves.

As we are met here to help each other to produce better work, and, as you will hear from others, as you have already heard, much useful information on the various crafts of a more or less technical and material nature, it is for us to kindle the thought and feeling that shall form the motive power by which material forces are to be turned to good account.

It is lamentable when men's minds are so absorbed by material conditions that they lose all sensibility to the higher forms of usefulness and happiness. Materialism alone is a demon of unrighteousness; one of its commonest effects is to belittle the faculty of reason, and allow our wills to follow the dictates of our emotions. We are content to be pleased with anything, without asking ourselves why. Things said to be charming are often accepted without question.

I have heard artists openly affirm that art has nothing do with reason. They say they are led in a mysterious way in their work, and never reason about it, although they talk reasonably enough about material qualities.

You can picture a world divorced from reason. Where for instance, would the emotion of love lead us without the guiding hand of reason? And that surely is our noblest emotion.

Our nature has always been twofold, viz, material and spiritual. And it is only common sense to recognise dual quality. We *must* distinguish between things which help to develop the body and those which lead to the purification and advancement of character.

When we speak of spiritual qualities we mean all mental and emotional conditions not necessarily of a religious nature. In these days of conflicting creeds it is rather desirable to foster spiritual activity outside the sphere of theology. Men of every class and every shade of religious belief recognise difference between thoughts and feelings that affect their hearts and characters, and thoughts and feelings which only affect their bodies.

Not for one moment would I belittle the importance of all material and bodily conditions. But in the cause of art and the higher qualities of man, we must pay more regard to the spirit and less to the flesh, without which spiritual basis no art is worth having at all. Personally, I feel that religion is essential to the healthy development of our spiritual nature. But I must not dwell on that side of the picture here.

The presence of so much ugliness in our life today is largely due to our materialistic habit of mind. We love ease far more than beauty, utility far more than inspiration; consequently 'ideas in things' are not readily recognised. Before going further, it is necessary to draw a clear distinction in our minds between associated ideas and intrinsic ideas. For instance, some have the idea that money is the root of all evil. This is an associated idea, due, we think, to reasoning. It is by the bad way in which money is used that evil is caused. But that is by the way. There is all the difference between such association and that inward intensity of feeling that produces an object, that will express spiritual qualities understood by those who see the object even for generations after the author is dead. Money can only be spoken of in this sense when the actual coins are considered as representing dignity, grace, refinement, reverence, etc. These ideas are intrinsic, not associated. And we shall often find the two kinds of ideas intermingled and overlapping, making it difficult to discern which is most potent. But the intrinsic are always more stable than the associated ideas. The latter are subject to change, but the former can never be.

All art is the expression or manifestation of thought and feeling; a technical knowledge of any craft by itself is but a language with which to express thought and feeling. And such qualities of mind as accuracy, order, neatness, precision, frankness, love of truth, and, above all, reverence, are some of the qualities of mind we call spiritual, because they minister to our characters far more than to our bodily comfort. We may make doors and windows, chairs and tables with mechanical exactness, and be paid in coin in exchange, but neither we nor those who pay for it will gain any spiritual benefit from our labour unless we have put our heart and minds into our work, anxiously seeking to impart some good thought and healthy feeling. Whether or not the workman be seeking to gain praise for himself or express praise of lovely qualities, will make all the difference to his influence through his productions. It will be vain and frivolous, or dignified, simple, and restrained. A thousand subtle feelings may be suggested by it according to the earnestness and purity of the man. It is base materialism to shut our eyes to the spiritual character given by man to matter.

Materialism has given rise to a thirst for artificial excitement. For in proportion to man's loss of interest in spiritual ideas, and in the manifestation of moral qualities, he loses enjoyment in his work, and cries out for amusement by itself. A workman to whom his work is a feast of reason and a flow of soul, does not want to waste much time on watching football matches; he is not hungry for the excitement of gambling; his joy is more constant and less spasmodic. I believe the old carpenters derived more pleasure from their work than we derive from ours, because they read less and thought more; putting more thought into their work, more thought was got out of it. Their ideas were fostered and stimulated by the thoughts and feelings in the things around them. The capital or door-knocker was eloquent in the appeal to their fancy. But now the idea that a chair or table can be made to express thought and feeling seems to our workmen quite ridiculous. Their thoughts are directed to collectivists' visions, votes, and public control of property; mundane considerations fill their horizon.

Differences in the material condition of men have existed ever since the world began, and I am not here to say if it is right or wrong that it should be so. But let us make quite sure that, however unequal the material condition of men, we all respond to the same virtues – love, reverence, humility, self-sacrifice, simplicity, truthfulness – all are understood, and loved by all. Thus we have a bond of union: whatever the differences may be in development, the spiritual qualities are to all alike a perpetual aim. Once let it be recognised that the spiritual verities are of primary importance, and that we can help on our own as well as our neighbours' growth in virtue by trying to put thought and feeling into our work, we shall then find an added joy in labour far more precious than any material reward. The delight of expressing thoughts and feelings which arouse interest and pleasure in others, is possible to every one of us. We are all endowed with the power to impart thought and feeling. All we need to acquire is the power to discriminate between good and noble thought and feeling and the baser sort. What have our schools done in this direction? What are they now doing? Many of them are teaching us that in certain past ages very beautiful work was done, and that such beauty is not possible to this dark age. We are all miserable sinners, so they say in effect; we must go on our hands and knees and measure up and draw and learn like parrots, to imitate with technical excellence what the ancient and good have showed us. My friends, this is false teaching. There is as much capacity for goodness today as there ever was in any age. Men can turn out work as perfect in all material qualities as the world has yet seen.

The difference between what is done now and what was done in years gone by, is due to spiritual qualities, not to material qualities. In the past men read and talked less, but thought and felt more. They had more pleasure in work and spent less time in games. They were more spiritual and less material in their attitude of mind.

The human quality in familiar objects has in many cases been driven out by the machine. Nevertheless, the machine has come to liberate men's minds for more intellectual work than was provided for them by the sawpit, though still there is much work in the world which requires little or no intelligence. Let us remember the sense of duty is yet left to us; and thousands will bear witness to the fact that the sense of duty has often transformed irksome tasks into pleasant labours. But, besides the comforting thought that the unpleasant labour is a duty, we shall find that many dull occupations may be made enjoyable by instilling spiritual qualities into them. Conscientiousness and a love of truth and hatred of all forms of deception will help us to make the hidden parts of our work as good as those that are seen. I do not think there is one here present who would not enjoy making our articles of furniture of one quality throughout, instead of oak in front and deal behind. And our patrons, if they, too, felt the same, would be glad to pay for the absence of sham. If we would frankly acknowledge the structural necessity of nailing down our floor-boards, we should not strain our ingenuity in devising methods of secret nailing. We are far too keen on mechanical perfection. That love of smooth, polished surfaces is very materialistic; it can be produced without brains, and in most cases can only be produced by the elimination of all human thought and feeling. It is delightful to see skill of hand and eye. All evidence of painstaking is a joy to behold. But in our materialism we have run after the perfection of the machine and preferred it to the perfection of the human heart. The modern builder will have the arrises of his stones drafted and made mechanically square and true, so that the mason can set them with plumb-rule and little or no thought, preferring that mechanical exactness to the work of the painstaking human eye. And, alas, many a mason prefers to use a tool rather than have to think. Thus is materialism encouraged on every hand.

You have all observed the soft, yet massive, effect in old buildings, when the angles were put up by human eye, and compared them with the hard, unsympathetic, mechanical effect of the modern drafted angle.

I would not have you go back to all methods of hand labour and neglect the aid of the Machine. All we need is to recognise its material value, and its spiritual imperfection, and put into all our hand-work that thought and feeling which is the breath of life. The worker and the worked-for all alike must co-operate to instil new life into all they make by dwelling on the moral and spiritual significance of things.

We are all keen enough if our local sanitation is at fault. We cry out loudly if a hospital settles down outside our door. Anything that endangers our body is at once attended to. But the hideousness of our lamp-posts, the poison to our souls' eyesight through the degradation of vulgar advertisements, is allowed to go on unhindered. We cannot hope to stem the torrent of hideousness all at once. Sensitiveness to beauty requires ages of cultivation, and can only spring from a deep and sincere love of truthfulness. To be true to your material, true to your conditions, true to your highest instincts, is the surest and only way to true art. So our first duty must be to sweep away all shams, and give up pretending to be Greeks or Romans in our architecture. If we have no noble ideas, let us hide our heads in the sand until we get some. But for pity's sake do not suppose that we are noble because we have learned how to copy the expressions of the noble men of old.

All the beautiful human work that has been bequeathed to us by the ages was the outcome of sincere and honest thought and feeling. And it is still those spiritual qualities that keep it alive in our affections today. Let us then see to it that our work is palpitating with sincere and noble thought and feeling, whatever our work may be. The frame of mind of the joiner in mitring his architraves is designed to have its effect, whether he be followed by the painter or not. Faithfulness in little things builds up the strong character and makes work enjoyable to the worker, and lays the foundation of that sense of beauty which we all need.

Reverence for nature is a fruitful source of beauty. Suppose the woman who wanted a bonnet were to recognise that her head was made by superhuman power, and out of reverence she ought to regard her bonnet as of secondary importance, her head being only lent to her, while her bonnet is her own; would she not come to think of the bonnet as a head *covering*, as something to protect her head, and so by considering fitness arrive at a reverend complement to nature? There was a striking article in *The Times* the other day, in which the writer advocated an attention to vocation in matters of dress. If people would dress more to fit them for their occupations, the modern costume would undoubtedly be more interesting and more fit, and, therefore, more beautiful. This is a subject worthy of more thought and attention than we can give it now. But it is only one of the many matters by which may be cultivated by both sexes that sincerity, and simplicity, and directness of purpose, which is the essence of all good work in whatever material we may be engaged with. This sincerity, simplicity, and directness we feel to be good, because fitness is a universal law of nature, and these qualities tend towards it, and it is also essential to beauty. The theory of evolution has disclosed the fact that all organisms are for ever moving in the direction of greater fitness and harmony of condition. It is as essential to fitness that objects should minister to our spiritual growth, as that they should minister to our bodily comforts and it is an important fact to which you will all assent, that only to minds set on goodness is the manifestation of beauty possible. That is to say, if our work is to be fit and beautiful, it must express some good thought or healthy emotion. Our homes must arouse the emotions of peace and goodwill.

Whatever we make, be it only a chair, can record our honest endeavour to serve a useful purpose, and stimulate kind feeling. Ruskin said, 'In old times men used their powers of painting to show the objects of faith; in later times they used the objects of faith that they might show their powers of painting'; and this exhibition of human skill has gradually usurped the place in man's affections that rightfully belongs to thought and feeling of a less material kind.

We make a great mistake in devoting all our attention to men's work. It is better to watch the ways of Providence than to copy the actions of men.

I am reminded of the mad hatter, when he put butter into his watch with a bread-knife. How our students think to ease their labours with the polish of Greece and crumbs of knowledge from Italy! When asked to design anything, we inquire how someone else did it; having no reverence for our contemporaries, we look to the dead and buried and find our museums crowded with lovely examples. Every inducement is held out to us to use the wits of others rather than our own. We even prefer to carpet our rooms with Eastern hieroglyphics, which we do not understand, rather than with patterns made at home. We imitate any foreigner rather than take the trouble to think for ourselves. Now, how does nature go to work? Everywhere we find her making the best possible use of immediate conditions, evolving beauty out of fitness and wisdom out of regard for requirements, materials and conditions all in exquisite harmony with established law. If we would go humbly to nature more, we should have a juster reverence for man's work. We should not be content to copy his successes and his failures, without exercising our own faculties. It is much more healthy for a student to be told the conditions and requirements necessary to provide any given object of use than to set him to copy the best example of the same in existence. The process of thought in the classification of requirements and conditions is immensely valuable. It stimulates the faculties and warms the heart, and encourages the feeling that there is room for improvement. But the general method of procedure is to fix on existing human production as more or less perfect and final, and superior to our own, and then copy, copy, copy, without having a full knowledge of all the circumstances and conditions that gave rise to the object of our admiration. The student's faculties are in this way cramped and petrified.

What we need is more reverent study of nature and nature's ways. The effect on the human mind of watching and tracing out the operations of nature is of untold value. It humbles a man and softens his judgments of his brother; it quickens all that is best in our characters. The more we look into nature, the more we feel the spiritual forces behind us all. It is this perpetual attention to the spirit in its purest manifestation that will improve our work, and so increase our happiness and usefulness. Ruskin says, 'All great art is the work of the whole living creature, body and soul, and chiefly of the soul.' The smallest article of daily life may be greatly enhanced in value by the spirit of the workman in its creation. It is quite easy to see when our articles of daily use are made by loving hands and thoughtful heads, and when they are made by human drudges working for wage alone. To impart this human spirit to anything, we must not imitate blindly; no feeling can be imparted until it has been truly felt by the workmen. This fact concerns us all, for we need to look for that spiritual feeling in objects which we wish to impart to our own productions. If I cannot be graceful and comely, I can at least have a graceful and comely umbrella, and in that way help to keep up my interest in those qualities.

It is a material necessity that we should specialise in various vocations. Life is so short. But we must not confound this specialising in various crafts and professions with the development of our spiritual nature. One man may work with a chisel and another with a brush, but both have the same human virtues to deal with. Both have the same spiritual qualities to think and feel about. Beauty in its myriad forms is not the prerogative of the painter. The expression of beautiful thought and feeling is the function of every

human creature and, for aught we know, every animal. It is a most mischievous distinction that has designated some men and women as artists, and led others to think that the expression of beautiful thought and feeling in things material is a matter they need not care or think about, or are incapable of understanding. It is universality of artistic expression and sympathy we need to encourage and foster, and which the attention to our spiritual nature will do more to stimulate than anything else. The added charm of mingling material and non-material, of living and working in the conscious light of spiritual ideas and feeling, must enrich the dullest labour. It surely is much more invigorating to believe that we are working to express universal ideas, than that our labours are purely material and perishable, appealing only to the lower part of man's nature. If also the spiritual quality is uppermost in our minds, we shall feel less the relative importance of our several occupations. We shall find spiritual giants in small, secluded places. A man's importance in the world will not be measured so much by his social position as by his earnestness. We cannot all be high priests, but we can all do much of the work of archbishops, if we like. At any rate, we must recognise that technical skill and material advantages carry us only a very little way in this world, and no way at all in the next. It is our spiritual fire that forces us onwards and upwards.

Let us now see how far these visionary ideas can he applied to everyday things. We pride ourselves on being such a hard-headed, practical nation. 'Utterly material' would be a more accurate description of us. It is quite common for people to remark, 'Oh, do look at that, did you ever see anything more hideous in your life?' but you never hear any one say, 'Oh, do go and inhale that foul odour, it is the worst you ever met with.' Why this difference? Surely it is because we all recognise that a bad smell is injurious to health or body; and in the former case we do not remember that ugliness is injurious to the health of our soul. Indeed, I fear some of you may not even admit my assumption. I am nevertheless convinced that if we paid more regard to spiritual matters, we should feel that all ugliness was to be avoided as a form of sin, and that it was as harmful to our characters as sewer gas is to our bodies. We should never look twice at what we believe to be ugly, any more than we would read of murders and divorce. If, then, we are to avoid all ugliness, we must be very simple in our homes and very careful not to harbour things that are intended to look better than they are. This striving for simplicity, if sincere, will enable us to distinguish between sensuous forms and colours and those things which stimulate the thought as well as the feeling of the beholder. It is very tempting placidly to enjoy mere sensuous effects and forget the much more valuable qualities that charm the mind as well as the heart. A great deal we collect around us is of that sensuous kind that causes purely emotional and vague feelings of pleasure, but leaves us no better than we were before. Lavish ornament is like a drug, the dose requires increasing as it loses its effect. But the moment you couple thought with sensuous feeling and healthy emotions, you feed the character and strengthen spiritual life.

We have, then, to bear this principle in mind in furnishing our homes. Let the simple articles of use show an honest endeavour to fulfil the practical purpose of their existence, and a reverent regard for the materials of which they are composed – that is, we must not use wood as if it were wrought iron, but suit our design to the natural character of the material. And let every bit of ornament speak to us of bright and healthy thought.

Do not string meaningless forms together merely for the purpose of sensuous pleasure. Better derive pleasure from the observation of fitness and proportion, because it is a nobler form of enjoyment – nobler, simply because it appeals to the whole man and not to the one faculty of sensation only.

We may learn something from the tree of the spirit of domestic happiness. We find the branches as they spring, radiating in

*ABOVE*: BOOKCASE AND STATIONERY CUPBOARD; *BELOW*: CABINET

rhythmic flow from the parent trunk, all harmoniously, not one on the top of the other in confused angularity; each bough and each twig grows a little to one side of those above and below, so that all can enjoy the sun and shower. This surely is brotherly love. Can we not get this feeling in our rooms by arranging our furniture and ornaments so that each has its due share, nothing being crowded, and every article helping to make its neighbour's virtue more, not less, pronounced. The essence of good proportion is brotherly love, making one line, surface, or space helpful to the full expression of another, in harmonious contrast, not angry rivalry.

The quickest thing in nature is a flash of lightning; it is made up of angles. So we find to give the effect of movement we require angularity of one kind or another. We call people crooked or cranky when they lack sweet reasonableness, and they show a want of stability that is disturbing. A stormy sea or sky is angular and cut up – the pained soul is said to be 'cut up'.

On the other hand, nature generally expresses the sweetest calm and repose. At sunset we see the horizontal lines as if all nature were reclining and preparing for rest, dim light drawing a veil over disturbing detail. Horizontalism thus suggests repose; it is the greatest contrast to angularity. These two opposite forms of angularity and horizontalism are the plainest statement of the opposite states of mind of disturbance and peace. Now when a friend enters your room and seems in doubt where to be seated, if he shows any signs of restlessness, be you very sure your room is at fault. But if he feels a half-conscious sense of repose, and is inclined to be peaceful, it will be in some measure because your room is not crowded with conflicting forms, colours, and textures.

The disturbance of the senses is often very subtle. You go to call on a friend; you leave the York stone pavement and stand on mosaic or tiles, then on coconut mat, then possibly, on polished wood, and then on pile carpet; all varying sensations in rapid succession, which are more or less destructive of repose according to the sensitiveness of the visitor. We do not need to be told that peace of mind is a desirable condition; therefore very little device we can bring to help us to that peace of mind which passes all understanding is good. This illustration is trivial enough, but it establishes a principle that in material things we can foster mental conditions by the aid of nature. How then can we get help from nature in the matter of colour? Grief and joy are expressed by our colours more than any other emotions. We find colours that stimulate and colours that soothe. We can produce the sensation of a drunken brawl by our combination of various coloured articles. Most of our drawing-rooms are of that type. Your eye is pitched from cushion to cushion like a hockey ball – the velvets, plushes, satins, silks, wools, cottons, marbles, metals, woods – it makes one's brain reel to mention the multitude – all trying to monopolise attention; not to speak of the so-called ornaments. Now what do we find nature doing? She furnishes with an abundance of the most soothing colour, viz, green; she uses her red most sparingly. In the spring she feasts us with delicate greens, greys, blues, purples, and, later on, yellow, gradually warming and strengthening her colour as the summer sun increases its power over the eye; and as our eyes and our senses are tiring, come the more stimulating oranges and browns, the deep, emphatic autumn colour. Then it is you hear people enthusiastic about ampelopsis and autumn tints generally. The more sensitive to colour have been enthusiastic all through the year. It takes a red flag to rouse John Bull.

One point we must all observe, whether we are very sensitive to colour or not. That is, that nature never allows her colours to quarrel. Her purple trees, with their gossamer of delicate spring green, dwell lovingly with the blue carpet of hyacinths. Harmony is everywhere. Nowhere without its dominating tint and jewel-like spots and patches of more brilliant colour. But the most brilliant colours are always in relatively small quantities. Nature never painted long lanes of brick-red. If you give her a chance she will bury your red with gold moss. It is the relative quantities of colour that make for harmony. Colours themselves are innocent enough. Like words, they need combining to demonstrate their worth. When nature is kindly treated and allowed healthy development, she shows her joy by purity of colour. Stir up the sediment of your pool and the mirror will no longer reflect truly, and so the idea of corruption is inevitably associated with impure colour.

One of the chief reasons why we should evolve our creations out of a due consideration of conditions and requirements, instead of imitating tradition or well-beloved examples, is that our conditions and requirements are always changing; new methods and new materials are constantly being evolved, and men's habits and tastes are for ever developing. What suited people of the last century is not quite in tune with the feelings and needs of our own time. If fitness is to be our law, as it is nature's law, we must not pin our conceptions to pre-existing forms too rigidly.

Any revivalism must involve the sacrifice of fitness. We should be ready to part with old traditions when we have found other methods more fit. We have certain characteristics peculiar to our own country and nation, such as climate, which we ought always reverently to acknowledge and rejoice in. Were we more spiritual, these conditions would be more respected and regarded as super-human. They would help us, rather than hinder us, to a fuller expression of the thoughts and feelings common to us all, and which, after all, are the main source of our real happiness and progress. It is by keeping alive and active these living faculties and continually polishing them up by sympathy and controversy, that we shall develop character and so beauty in the world.

One of the commonest and yet the most precious feelings we all have is that of generosity. We admire the bounty of the wealthy, but how much more do we delight in the generosity of the poor. How different are the mediums of generous feeling. Ruskin told us the greatest charity was the giving of praise. Certainly it is more tonic to the praiseworthy than much fine gold. But it is the effect of generosity on the giver to which we wish now to draw attention, for in the feeling of generosity we have a very powerful influence for good which affects our works in a marvellous manner. Unfortu-nately, it is more often a quality we look for in others than in ourselves. But it is one that affects every craft and every produc-tion. The feeling that we must bestow some benefit, give to others something we believe to be good. If this feeling were more cultivated it would tend to greater enjoyment of life to all of us. This spiritual quality is stifled by over-attention to material gain. The carpenter in making a door for us will think he has served us better by adding an eighth of an inch of thickness more than he bargained for than if he strove to think and feel and show a keen desire to express dignified and simple proportion, faithful care in the hidden parts, and an earnestness to serve well and assist the efforts of brother workmen. That spiritual frame of mind is nonetheless real because we cannot gauge it with a foot rule. How often, indeed, metaphorically speaking, we measure out our wood and labour and balance it with the payment we are to receive; but in nowise does the bestowal of anything come into our reckoning – and therein lurks the great question of life. Wood and labour we can measure and weigh; but if in addition to material and labour we add thought and feeling, we are bestowing just that spiritual quality which will make our wood and labour a joy to producer and possessor alike. Is not this thought and feeling, then, the very soul of material creations, and the only enduring quality about them? Is it not because we believe the pursuit of beauty tends to improve character that we are so keen about the arts? Or perhaps we are ordained to derive pleasure from beauty because it is elevating to the soul. So we are led by natural instincts to seek that which will improve our condition, both material and spiritual. But, although so precious, it cannot take the place of the material qualities or be made manifest without matter; thus we have still to be careful to give the material qualities we are paid for; and in our care we are bestowing a certain amount of that very thought and feeling we regard as essential. We thus show an anxiety to be just and to avoid taking more than our due. So by the very nature of things we cannot escape from spiritual considerations. It rests with us to stimulate and enrich this quality by the addition of generous feeling, and in so doing add the thought and feeling that will make our work something more than the mere fulfilment of material requirements. The door, then, may be a joy and even an inspiration; it may express welcome, grace, dignity, simplicity, and arouse interest; it may soothe and solemnify or irritate and vex you. You pass through it with feelings of pleasure or of pain, or with no feeling at all. But the point for us to consider is, what has the maker of it gained and given by his labour? Has he polished up his own and our thought and feeling? If he endeavoured to do his best and gave a little more thought and feeling in the making than he was paid for, then has he truly enriched his own character and all those of us who take the trouble to observe his work with care; and if we lived in a less material state of mind we should be more entertained by the observation of each other's work. It is unfortunate that we only observe the work of those that the newspapers call out about, and then often only superficially.

We frequently find the instinct to enrich exercised in adding only material qualities. As, for instance, the door may be moulded and chamfered, and have bevelled panels, innumerable crevices and ledges for dust, which in no way minister to our thoughts and feelings except to distress them with a sense of wasted labour – labour not only in the making, but in the keeping clean. Such so-called enrichments are not real enrichments at all, though they add to the complexity and intricacy of anything. Unless they add to our pleasures, they are so much waste, not to say poison. If, on the other hand, by our mouldings and panellings we arouse the sense of grace, proportion, dignity, delicacy or greater fitness, we are certainly enriching our work. And these qualities can be made manifest only by our earnestly feeling them.

Think what a keen love of cleanliness could do if applied to our architecture in dirty towns. How much so-called ornamental enrichment collects dirt and depresses us by harbouring all that is unclean and repulsive – producing feelings the very reverse of pleasure. The very proper pleasure we feel in dexterity is often sacrificed for the sake of elaborate ornamentation that is hopelessly meaningless and sometimes used to hide bad workmanship and bad material. This kind of enrichment gives no pleasure, and cannot stimulate any nice feeling or healthy thought.

We cannot be too simple. A true desire to be simple strengthens our sense of fitness, and tends to the perfecting of proportion and workmanship, and a more reverent regard for the natural qualities of material. Carving richly veined marbles and finely figured woods is only the action of irreverence and conceit. We ought to respect nature's veining too much to allow of our chopping it up with man-made pattern. We are too apt to furnish our rooms as if we regarded our wallpapers, furniture, and fabrics as far more attractive than our friends. We don't mind how a hideous chimney-piece destroys the outline of our human heads and protrudes its complex gathering of forms, colours, and textures in distressful restlessness, catching our eye at every glance and robbing us of that calm we need wherewith to see into the soul of our companion. In this climate the fireplace should be the centre of interest in a room, when considered as an apartment. But in actual life it is subservient to human beings, pictures, sculpture, or books, or anything else possessing more thought and feeling. It is the thought and feeling alone by which we must classify the things around us.

Often the feeling of generosity is expressed by making the parts of a building or object larger than may be actually required on structural grounds. For instance, the old roofs were composed of massive timbers, it being in old time often cheaper to use a whole tree than cut it up. There is a certain satisfaction to the eye to be gained by proportions which are in excess of mathematical requirements. We call the architect's work an art, but the engineer's work a profession; and the difference may be traced to just that addition of the spiritual quality of generosity, just that thought and feeling which humanises the work. The engineer's labour satisfies us on account of its fitness; it appeals to our intellect rather more than to our heart.

Of course, the association of ideas is a very important factor in the formation of our taste, and must often be the chief groundwork on which we build up our principles of design. For instance, the ocean illustrates perpetual motion, and nature contrasts with it the horizon as if to steady our contemplation. It is obvious the wave lines and forms give movement, while angularity suggests violent action. The lightning flash we have already alluded to. When the storm rages, does it not hide the horizon, and so increase the sense of violent action?

Would that we more often thought of this principle in our house-building. Looked at from every point of view, most of our houses resemble the forms of storms. Hardly anywhere do we see houses standing peacefully as if to stay and calm you by their reposeful-ness. They look more like spectres that came and went in the twinkling of an eye, angularity and infinite variety of shapes and proportions jutting out at you with surprising wildness as if they were waving their arms impatiently and angrily; and to add to their complexity they are composed of an infinite number of differently coloured materials and textures, just like the drawing-rooms inside, which I likened to drunken brawls. It is our mad rush for wealth and material things that feeds on advertisement, until our very houses shout at us for attention.

A little more love of peace and quietness and a greater readiness to take a seat behind nature, instead of crushing her under our feet, will help to make our buildings more pleasing and restful. Greater spirituality, in fact, should blot out all material vulgarities. Our wonderful resources for gaining knowledge and culture has not made our work more beautiful. The most intimate knowledge of the history of Greece and Rome, what has it done for our buildings? It has failed hideously, and stimulated pride in scholarship. It has made us vain, but not thoughtful; arrogant, but not emotional. Better had we sought out the immortal thoughts and feelings that guided the spirits of ancient times.

Materialism has been the seed we have sown, and we have only tares to reap. Or let us say, we are at the end of a hideous night, and now awakening to the necessity of sowing living seed. All around are signs of renewed activity and reaction from materialism.

Whether you be architects or craftsmen of any sort, you are all interested in home life; so I now invite you all to fancy you are architects, and commissioned to build me a home. Shall I tell you of some charming villa, say in Italy, or Kamschatka, that I have seen and liked. Shall I dwell on my own taste, and so control your actions and feelings; because I am paying you, must you be my humble servant? No! My dear architects, let me rather marry your spirits to my own, and see what broad principles of thought and feeling are there already, to work in unison with me – affections common to all men. I will be no slave-driver, but we will work together for good. A united effort on our part to express the best thought and feeling, and foster the noblest ideas, will surely tend to the production of more good than if, with perfect taste, imposed thoughts and feelings upon you, or for one moment forgot that you had a conscience to obey as tender as my own.

We have only £3,000 to spend on land and building; we have to be in easy reach of a railway, and live with constant thought for economy of time and money. We have a site with trees on undulating ground. The view to the north-west is lovely. But the main road is also on the north-west. Will it not then be better for soul and body to capture the early morning sun, which is never too hot in England, and is a great purifying influence, rather than allow the beautiful view to direct the placing of our rooms? A view can be enjoyed out of doors; it is surely second in value to the sunshine. The latter is very inspiring, and will cheer the sad spirit at breakfast, much more than the view. And it is in the early morning that the spirits of the hyper-sensitive and physically weak need the encouragement of sunshine. So we surely all agree that that which most contributes to spiritual health is the most desirable. We then have fixed a south-east or east aspect, and our prospect will be best from our hall, or staircase, or passages, on the north-western side of the house, where we are more often passing along than resting. No one in his senses will sit for hours in the house, looking at the view he has every day, no matter how beautiful it is. But it does us all good to have the stimulating joy of a good view intermittently, and for a short time. We enjoy it more if so presented to us.

Our next care in fixing the position of the house is that we should show no want of reverence for trees or natural levels of ground. We can never build anything half as beautiful as a tree; and we agree that human reverence for nature is not a quality to be despised, so we will choose our ground with due regard to all upon it. And for the sake of simplicity and repose, select the most level part. You will express decision and determination by forming a straight path or drive from the road to the house, making it wide to suggest hospitality and welcome, and avoiding any wobbling indecision, which only suggests weakness.

Our need for economy will keep us near the entrance boundary, that is, the north-western side; our love of privacy, which is very much a matter of temperament, may be a good reason for leaving little or no garden between the house and the road. On a small site the entrance must be very evident, and overlooks the whole area on the roadside of a house. You may not quite share my love of privacy, but if I ask for it to be considered, even if some may think it a weakness, I shall not be asking you to violate your consciences.

Let our love of privacy be encouraged into reticence, and, let our building play into the hands of nature. As a sympathetic accompanist, both in colour and form, we can show a desire to be subdued and quiet and restful, modestly hiding behind trees, if possible, and not towering into the air to look down on them with scorn. We may be sure that all who behold our countryside will regard our building, whatever it be, as of second importance to the natural scenery, and will be most grateful to us if we do not mar their enjoyment. It will affect our design materially if we both feel a desire not to hurt the feelings of any beholder. A jagged, angular outline against the sky, a forest of chimney-stacks, or roofs of purple slate edged with pink binding, complicated, intricate masses piercing every space – there is no end to our power to disturb and excite our fellow-creatures; and we do it often quite needlessly from want of thought and because we do not believe that sincere desire not to be noisy and restless will help us when we are designing. Furthermore, a feeling for simplicity and restfulness will result in economy of labour and material, and perhaps leave us with a little spare cash to devote to one spot of sculpture, one point of pre-eminent interest in which we might suggest some merriment like the old grotesques. If, however, we use figure sculpture, let it not be a gentleman without his hat, or a lady with nothing on. For in this climate such exhibitions only excite our pity and discomforting sympathies. Hence the severe convention that the old workers always adopted. If the material selected to represent our merry thought is handled with due regard to its intrinsic nature, we shall be helped to feel that the image is only stone or wood or lead, or whatever it be, invested with ideas – in short, a symbol, the idea of which so dominates that our pity is not aroused. The more materialistic our minds, the more realistic our art. Realistic rendering of material qualities should only be allowed so far as is absolutely necessary for the force of spiritual expression. For the sake of repose, let it be at rest, and not representative of perpetual or sudden action. All workers associate home with the idea of rest. Repose, we hope for, even in the vilest cockney villa. Then must we surely try to suggest in our building the possibility of gaining our heart's desire.

So you will gather your flues together, and collect the rooms in such sequence that will enable you to cover them with one roof, or as few roofs as possible.

Planes at varying angles catch and cut up the lights and shades and add to complexity, to the destruction of repose and breadth.

If I am wrong in desiring simplicity and repose, and you honestly feel it to be wrong, your clear and only duty is to throw up the commission, for we are at variance on one of the main principles which is going to affect our action throughout the entire building and its furnishing. But supposing we are agreed in the belief that the highest developments of character are only possible under peaceful and simple conditions of mind, that war and turmoil are only the extreme conditions of a want of repose and simplicity – then it is obvious that the home should be the most peaceful, restful, simple servant we possess. And we will run our thoughts over the whole place to see wherein ideas in harmony with and conducive to these feelings can be reasonably manifested. My architect will gladly join with me in warm welcome to friends, and kindly sympathetic thought for domestics. That will make us hesitate to spend an undue amount of money on entrance hall and reception-rooms, which would necessitate shabby quarters for servants, and greater pretence to luxury and display than our means could sustain. The visitor must not be disappointed when he becomes intimate, and is allowed into the more private parts of the house. The wide door, like the arms we open to receive our friends, is right and suggests generous feeling, but more than sufficient height in our door only gives the idea of magnificence, which would only lead to disappointment if the rooms, for economy, are low. The same character and scale must be observed throughout, from the beginning to the remotest corner. We need to be consistent, to be sincere. Neatness and order we require in every detail, because they are associated with precision and order of mind, the keeping of appointments and prompt attention to engagements – faithfulness, in fact. These are habits of mind greatly encouraged by neatness and order. And to suggest these qualities few materials are more effective than many.

If the money at our disposal will not pay for oak joinery everywhere, then let us have it nowhere. It is far more durable than painted deal, and more expensive in the first instance; therefore to have the entrance and reception-rooms in oak, and the rest deal, at once suggests the 'whited sepulchre'. As Augustus Welby Pugin said of the dissenting chapel-builders of his day, 'And then they thought the Lord to cheat by building the back parts shabby.' If we are to encourage our carpenters and bricklayers to be conscientious in their work in hidden places, we must set them the example by designing our house to have every part of equal quality, so far as is consistent with the use of each part. That is, fitness must be studied. But it would not be consistent with fitness to use deal in my kitchen that I might have oak in my hall; it would be regarded by some as mere vulgar display. One little jewel-like spot of stained glass would be better than any great expanse of material more costly than the average material used throughout the building.

My architect will give me ventilation and a system by which the air of my rooms is kept slowly moving, thus avoiding draughts. He will not make my rooms high, and thus deceive me into thinking them healthy. Height must be controlled by the length of my rooms. Because we are seeking to produce the feeling of repose, low rooms will help us greatly, and give us the benefit of reflected light, and allow of smaller windows. You will tell me, small windows, when rightly placed, in conjunction with white ceilings and friezes, may produce very light rooms, and have the advantage of preserving equable temperature throughout the year. You will so

*ABOVE*: VOYSEY LIVING ROOM AS EXHIBITED IN THE ARTS AND CRAFTS EXHIBITION, 1896; *BELOW*: CHESTERFIELD, c1907

save me the expense of elaborate blinds and curtains, and give me all the sun I need without the scorching or glare on the hottest summer days; again simplifying not only the furnishing of my rooms, but the cleaning and warming of them.

It is pleasant to feel well protected when the weather is disturbed and angry; so you will not give me great sheets of plate glass, which look like holes in the walls both from within and from without. I much appreciate your regarding me, and suggesting to others that I am to be regarded as a precious thing, to be protected from all violent intrusion.

We like, on entering a house, to see our wants anticipated. A warm fire in the hall is akin to a warm welcome. You will provide a lavatory for coats and hats, boots etc, so that mud need not be taken upstairs – as we feel that coats and hats without a soul inside are distressful objects, so they should be stowed away out of sight.

The same material for my entrance hall and lavatory floors will save me the sensation of change and loss of repose; and it will be comforting to feel I am doing no damage before my hob-nailed boots are taken off.

You will think of my taste for music and give me bells each with its individual voice, to be rung with wire in the old-fashioned way, so that through them we may express our feelings and denote our personality. The electric ring only stabs without revealing the assassin: it cannot call like a bell.

The number of servants kept and the extent of my family we may assume you to be aware of; such are purely material conditions that are of great importance, but may be omitted for the moment, while we are considering the less material character of the home.

It is desirable to so plan the house, if it is not too small, that the servants shall enjoy the same freedom to be reasonably merry as I wish to enjoy myself. My noise should be shut off from them, as theirs is from me. The laughing and talking in which one does not participate is not always pleasant. But my architect will find it hard to give me that quality, if I am not very generous. So if I am ungenerous with my money, it behoves me when in the house to be very generous in my sympathy, and bear the noisy servant with patience. Double doors and double windows are delightful harbingers of quiet. But am I reasonable in expecting such expensive qualities for the amount I have to spend? And will not greed show his ugly face in my house if I ask for too much? If you be my friends, you will check my greediness. Many must suffer if it is allowed to prevail, and then all sorts of nasty ideas will appear. The sitting and dining rooms may be likened to human heads. The door is the mouth, through which many good things may pass. The windows are the eyes, through which we may see the beauties that are superhuman, and the fireplace is the heart of the room, or the countenance of the whole face. If it is a well fire, low down and dejected, it looks cringing and lazy. But if it is high up above the hearth, it seems standing as a good servant ready for service. Here I am, it says, ready to warm all who come near; I am not trying to hide my head in the ashes. Behold my wide, open mantelpiece, broad and simple as if to make room for many. The natural flame and flicker and smoke are so rich and lively in their movement, all the arts of man cannot compete with such form and colour; so my reverent architect will take very good care not to oppose his hand-made lustres and elaborate combinations of textures and colours that will rival the fire's charms and make us indifferent to both in the end. The idea that the burning wood or coal is the centre of the interest in the fireplace, and that grate and hearth and fender and fire-irons all its humble servants, need not prevent these accessories from being pregnant with delicate grace and lively thought and feeling. All we ask is that they be reticent and unassertive in colour; never for a moment put into competition with the super-human fire; and I don't want to be frightened out of my life by having a hearth that will break if I by accident drop the poker.

You will so proportion my fireplaces to their rooms that where I enjoy the company of my family and friends, there shall be ample room for all to gather round, and feel the moment they enter that there is room. It is painful to enter a room and feel you are disturbing any one. This feeling can be avoided by you, if I allow you to build and furnish my home. If all I care about is the needs of the flesh, I shall save a lot of thought and feeling by handing over my home to a universal provider to be furnished and equipped. All the thinking that will be needed will be to tell him what foreign style or ancient period he is to follow. And even that amount of thought I may save myself, as it is only one of price. If we fix that, Mr Upholsterer will do all the rest. But why should we turn the house into a co-operative store, and advertise everybody's mustard and credulity, when all the while my architects are bursting with thoughts and feeling that people read novels and go to churches and theatres to think about, because they have not got attractive ideas in their own homes? Here, in this hall, are the same elements that have written volumes in stone and wood, glass and painting, and all literature besides. We only need to turn the current of our energies on everyday articles of use, and they shall speak to us of beautiful thoughts and feelings, as they spoke to our forefathers in the 13th and 14th centuries.

With this difference, that we have changed our mode of life, and many methods of work, many materials and material advantages have been discovered which must change our forms, but need not change our feelings. The love and protection of home has not, or should not have died out with battlements. We have now to protect our homes from the onslaught of the fraudulent, the insincere, the gross, and the ugliness of thoughtlessness and animalism. I need you to barricade my doors not against battering rams, but against the poison of pretentious ornament and elaborate shams.

Will you help me show my respect for local conditions of climate and soil, not ignoring altogether the modern facilities of transit, but as far as possible selecting your material to harmonise with local character in colour and texture? For instance, can there be any harm in using green slate from Wales or Cumberland in counties that produce no slate, considering that the green slate is far more harmonious with nature than red tiles, and makes a more durable roof? Then, again, you will tell me oak was once the most durable and plentiful building wood in England. Now we can get it from Austria better seasoned but much softer. It is more quickly grown than English oak, and therefore easier to work, but not so beautiful; and the latter is hard to get well seasoned. Our habits of looking for material excellences, fine finish, smooth, polished surfaces and perfect workmanship, has made us shy at English oak joinery, when it opens at the joints, cracks, and winds and gets uneven. Are we right in adopting the French taste for French polish in this way? I think not, and give you leave to pardon any roughness, provided it is due to natural causes and not to man's carelessness or fraud.

In old time, when the carriage of materials was more costly, local material was more used, and only the vain rich made use of imported material. Vain we call them, because we think it was vanity of wealth or travel that led them to such display. And so we have come to notice and be greatly charmed by the characteristic colour and texture in the old buildings of different districts. There is a harmony in nature's materials both in colour and texture, and you notice it among the peasants of some counties still: their eyes and their dress harmonise with the colour of the rocks and soil, and are eloquent in their appeal to our sense of fitness. It is when you get near great towns you find materialism more pronounced than spirituality. Then all sorts of influences of a material nature come in to destroy the intuitive grace of the ignorant peasant, as if Providence forced us to develop our own faculties by withdrawing our intuitions where opportunities for self-culture were more abundant, so leaving us to feel that we have to find out the laws of harmony and beauty for ourselves. We have begun by floundering,

BOLTS & BITS, TAKEN FROM THE THOMAS ELSLEY & CO, PORTLAND METALWORKS CATALOGUE

but we are in health, because we are conscious of and dissatisfied with our floundering.

You, my good architects, can help to steady my tottering by your manly defence of those ideas and feelings, which you feel within your own breasts, and know to be of universal esteem. The repose and breadth of the rooms I leave you to arrange as I ask for no cornices which produce lines of shade, no ornament on my ceiling which I cannot look at without paining my neck – ornamental ceilings are fit only for large rooms and halls. Then with deep frieze and picture-rail high enough to take pictures of the right size for my rooms, the utmost effect of length and width will be given to each room, which in a small house is more valuable than height. By omitting the cornices you avoid emphasising the height of the rooms, and you also omit so many dust traps. To some minds the very absence of these things suggests cleanliness and order. I want no finger-plates, because they suggest dirty fingers in my house.

You will arrange my rooms with their furniture so that each piece has the place most suited for its use, with light helping to make it more useful, so that we feel no single bit of furniture is quarrelling with or harassing another, and everything shall have its useful purpose. Thus proportion and grace and the intention to serve a useful purpose will provide the very best elements of beauty, and ornaments will be little required. If you give me one or two in each room, such as pictures and sculpture, they will be infinitely more impressive when alone than when in a crowd. You cannot listen to two people talking at the same time, so we don't want a thousand ornaments to be bawling at us all day long. The fewer ornaments you give me, the more keenly I shall demand that each shall be of high quality. Again we feel that simplicity involves perfection. The more simple the ornament, the better must be its proportion, the more graceful and the more noble its appeal to my mind and heart. By your great discrimination you enhance the value of the artist's work, you draw special and careful attention to it, and allow it to engage undivided attention, which is far kinder to all concerned than plastering the walls with lovely pictures from floor to ceiling, giving the effect that I was infinitely proud of my wealth, and infinitely indifferent to my friends' enjoyment. I would rather delight you with the contemplation of one ornament, than weary you with a museum full, however beautiful the objects might be. Museums are places for special study, and when used as such are most valuable.

When you design my tables and chairs, you will think of the machine that is going to help in the making, and choose such shapes as are easily worked by machinery. When labour was cheap and men uneducated and less fit for more intellectual work, the legs and arms of tables and chairs were charmingly curved and formed by hand into fanciful shapes, and delight us still with their human subtlety. But now, alas, your wood comes to you machine-sawn and machine-planed, and the only thought and feeling you can put into your furniture must be through a mechanical medium. So right proportions and the natural qualities of the wood, the suitable colour and texture of the upholstery make up your limited vocabulary. You can tell me if the master and mistress have a sufficient sense of importance to give themselves high-back armchairs to dine in, while their family and friends have low backs and no arms. If all had high backs, by the way, it would be difficult for the waiters, unless the chairs were very wide apart.) This idea of the importance of host and hostess is not to be despised; it is closely related to ceremonial of all kinds, and ceremony was always associated with kingship, and kingship with self-control. The origin of the crown, you remember, was to symbolise self-control by the binding round, controlling, and confining of the head with a band or ring. It was believed once that self-control was the first and essential quality for the control of others. The nimbus of the saint first of all denoted this quality, until men became materialistic, and then self-control was translated into power and glory. Crowns are now used to denote splendour. If I give splendid pecuniary assistance to my political party, they will procure for me a splendid crown. Then shall you address me as Your Lordship. But first you must be lord over me; that is, guide and control my affections, and express the better side of my nature, as in harmony with the better side of your own. You may find the ceremonial ideas dependent on my social position in a great measure; but not wholly. Wealth fixes social position in our days, but breeding or heredity settles instincts. So you have to find out if I have a taste for putting on my boots in the dining-room or not, and many other little habits which are fairly innocent and in no way material to the moral and spiritual verities that we are most concerned with. The less attention is drawn to class differences, the better; so I shall leave it to you to suit your designs to my little idiosyncrasies, remembering, as you will do, that the vital thoughts and feelings are common to all, and if there is a difference it is only one of degree.

Enough has been said to lead you to introduce ornament, that is, machine-made mouldings and pattern and decoration of any kind, only when it is needed on practical grounds, such as the moulding of a skirting board to avoid the wide ledge for dust at the top, or the rounding, splaying, or moulding of exposed angles, or the emphasising of horizontalism with a view to suggest repose, or the binding together of points of interest by strings of moulding, delicate lines that express unity and rhythm. You will naturally concentrate the effect of richness and focus the attention on those objects that have most to say to us, things which appeal most readily and profoundly to our thoughts and feelings; you will hesitate to waste mouldings on places and things, when the addition of such can add no interest and no joys. The mere effect of meaningless elaboration is called by some the effect of richness. But we want real richness, not the effect of it. And real richness is not possible without thought and feeling. Miles of machine-made mouldings cannot arouse a moment's pleasant thought or feeling.

The effect of real richness is only obtainable by having precious materials, elaboration concentrated and harmoniously arranged, and eloquent with thought and feeling.

Your attention to this principle is going to affect your design of every detail, including spoons and forks. It leads to the full use of the individual characteristics of the different materials we are using, so that interests gained by the observation of natural qualities, and is not dependent on artificial elaboration. The full force of our thought and feeling not coming into competition with nature, but added to it only in certain places. Everything we have to handle may be so fashioned as to show indifference to our feelings or a desire to please. It will either attract or repel our touch.

We do not run to embrace the hedgehog, nor does any one desire to wring the neck of an apostle – yet we find the apostle on the handle of spoons. The significance of which – but for our demand for fitness – we should be expected to applaud. But as a handle it is no better than our fire-irons, door knobs, knockers, and innumerable other things we have to touch, which are cast and chased or wrought in rugged irregularity, as much to say, if you come near me you shall be stabbed and bruised; instead, the idea of friendliness and loving help could be suggested by making all our handles not only pleasant to feel, but looking attractive to feel. The same may be expected of caskets, inkstands, ash-trays, and everything that we have to touch. Your desire to serve me well and avoid paining me must help to convey pleasant thoughts and feelings.

You have my guest chamber to arrange. Will it not charm the visitor more, to find every little want anticipated, writing and reading provided for him so that he may retire and yet be entertained, if he so desires it, rather than to find his room a perfect reproduction of the bedchamber of a foreign potentate? If my friend be an archaeologist, no doubt at first he will be overjoyed to find a room of revived antiquities, but may end by swearing because he cannot find a button hook. But if the room be of the former type, will he not exclaim, 'Oh, bless mine host!' and go down to dinner with an appetite?

In olden time, when people believed in knights and fairies, the four-post bedstead suggested protection while you slept, and gave an air of solemnity and importance to the bed which was once regarded as the soul of the bedchamber. But since then the sanitary expert has come along, and in his craze for perfect physical conditions, he made us all believe we needed more fresh air than our forefathers, and iron and brass bedsteads were found to be capable of glitter and tawdry effect. They were cold homes for insects and inhospitable alike to them and all who liked glowing thoughts. The designers were so cold-blooded that they arranged metal balls conveniently high to chill your hands upon. The one idea was air space – air space. Are prophets and poets bred on air space? If not, what is?

The proper ventilation of the bedroom and healthy conditions of rest do not entirely depend on air space or metal bedsteads. Indeed, the old fourposter was much more calculated to inspire right thoughts and feelings, and in a properly ventilated bedroom is as healthy and clean as any metal atrocity.

Another important element you will have to consider is the carpets. I will not ask you to provide them with pattern, because pattern hides dirt. The fact that dirt is merely hidden ought only to satisfy the ostrich. He is the gentleman, I believe, who thinks he is not seen when his head is hidden in the sand. We have already come to the conclusion that pattern to be worth anything must contain thought and feeling; so the floor is hardly the place to look for it, unless it be in a small mat that is not cut up by furniture. Besides, we must remember that the floors, like the walls, are backgrounds to things of greatest interest and importance. And therefore the pattern, if we have any, should not interfere with the attractiveness of the objects seen against it. That is, if we want to avoid quarrelsome, noisy confusion. Remember you are considering an average man's home. There are places, of course, where handsome and elaborate floors and ceilings are most fit. The Persians have shown us what perfection the carpet may be capable of, but they have also shown us how to use it when made. They do not cover it with little tables of plush, and use it as background to museum and bazaar articles.

Much that we have been considering is not applicable to the rich man's palace or public building. When speaking of the fireplace many of you will have recalled the exquisite examples of richly carved and emblazoned chimney-pieces in which the symbolic interest of the decoration is made of greater importance than the fire by reason of its being charged with human thought and feeling, making it in some measure a more intellectual treat to behold than the first which arouses a material and sensuous kind of pleasure.

In like manner magnificence of all kinds was excluded by my poverty. My station in life must determine your indulgence in the rendering of ideas most fit and harmonious. You will not hang around my hall the dead heads of wild beasts, unless you think me a bloodthirsty murderer, vain of my killing powers; and even then your better natures would check your encouragement of my vice.

Let natural qualities strike the keynote of your design. If you are building a garden pool – think first of the water, its crystalline quality and reflecting power, which will be strengthened by having a dark material as a background or lining, so emphasising the chief charm of the water, and showing a proper reverence for its natural beauty. But on the other hand you would provide a washhand basin with inside as pure white as you can find, because with a small quantity of water that will accentuate the transparency and purity which attract one to wash in it.

It is in this way we should reverently follow nature's suggestions, and not be absorbed by our own sensuous likes or dislikes of certain colours and textures.

If, then, in building for me you find so many conditions and feelings to be thought of and served, every one you have to work for must in like manner furnish you with similar conditions, varying as the personality varies. And if we will respect all these variations in character and temperament, it will add enormously to our pleasure and interest in the work of life.

Drumming and drilling human beings into the same conventional mould is madness and folly.

Instead of studying the five orders of architecture, we had far better study the five orders of Englishmen: The really noble, the would-be noble, the cannot-be noble, the sometimes noble, and the half noble. As Pope said, 'The proper study of mankind is man.' This would give immense vitality to our work, and we should feel the perpetual progress of the immortal spirit of things. It is enervating to dwell perpetually on dead and perishing materials. We instinctively recoil from all ideas of decay, and rejoice in the permanence and stability of nature's laws; and so we try to build with imperishable material and select all those that are most lasting. This quality of permanence and stability is only relatively possible in the material world. But it is the very life of the spirit. The idea of durability is one we will sacrifice much to convey.

The use of animal life is dependent on our spiritual activity. If we are thoroughly materialistic, we prefer fruit and flowers in our wallpapers and fabrics, and feel hurt by the mutilation of birds or animals when cut round furniture or upholstered on to seats. But if the rendering of animals in our decoration is so conventional that we feel only that the spirit of the beast is recorded, no pain is felt. The martlet in heraldry never pained any one, but a very realistic bird with all its feathers carefully drawn and its legs cut off would pain us at once, the dominant impression or idea being, a very material bird injured, mutilated, and maimed. While, in the case of the martlet, the illustration is of the bird spirit; it is a generic bird, not any particular species. And our thought is kept in the region of spiritual rather than material realities. It would be well if this distinction could be understood and appreciated more generally, because there is a vast amount of prejudice against the introduction of animal forms in our decoration which is entirely due to our materialistic attitude of mind. Materialism has been the cradle of realism in art. The life of animals might be made a source of stimulating joy to our own lives. We all feel a sense of pleasure when the wild birds sing, and the idea of their love-making and aspiring and growing more good and useful every day is delightful, and ought to be recorded in our everyday articles of use, as well as in our natural history books. What is it that makes us all delight in Shakespeare's work? Is it not his own spiritual delight in spiritual ideas: in life, in thoughts and feelings, rather than in things?

You shall perch four eagles on my bedposts to drive away bad spirits, as the Byzantines believed, and rest my fire-irons on the backs of brass cats, not dogs, for cats are the most faithful fireside dwellers. On my table let there be fruit and flowers and one or two *symbolic* animals, and let the foods be handed round. A boiled potato is not inspiring, however well it may be served; and, moreover, the momentary glance at food is more appetising, therefore it is better on a side table.

The living, conscious life is far more healthy to dwell upon than anything that is dead or lifeless. So we desire to add thought and emotion to all things around us.

A well-known paint manufacturer told me the other day that when his men brought him a new colour or new mixing they were pleased with they always spoke of it as 'she'. 'Isn't she a beauty?' they would say; showing their pleasure and interest in their work led to their endeavour to invest it with spiritual significance, to give it a personality. Surely it is a natural instinct to attach spiritual ideas to the materials that please us. Were this feeling more common we should be less led away by fashions in things.

In lighting by day and by night, invite you to bestow much care. The essential idea suggested by light is activity, and the chief material consequence is cleanliness. We all like abundance of light for work or play. It stimulates action. But we do not want windows that have to be covered up by the upholsterer morning, noon, and night. Precious as the light is, we must not be blind to the soothing mystery and charm of shadow and twilight. The suggestions of repose and mystery are sublime, and as necessary as the brilliant light. To light up an ordinary room all over at night is to destroy all sense of repose. Again observe nature, how she lights by day and by night. There is always one dominating point most brilliant and never more than one, attended by countless degrees of subordinate brilliancy in reflections around it. The old builders understood the value of a dim religious light far better than this materialistic age. So in my dining-room you can suggest by your method of lighting the splendour of my guests and the richness of flowers and fruits on my table, while contrasting them with the solemn mystery of the gloom all round the room. When I look across the table into the faces of my family I do not want to see them confused with ornaments, and furniture of any kind behind them, but to behold the guardian angels hovering in the shade, or the glittering haloes that my good spirit may perceive.

We have alluded to many trivial details of domestic life, believing that great ends have small beginnings, and that if the thin end of the wedge of spiritual significance can be driven in among the common objects of life, it will raise our interest and stimulate our higher nature and lead to noble thought and feeling by which we hope to advance in character and conduct and brighten many a dark place in this vale of tears.

The only instruction I have, then, to give you, amounts to this: Think of the needs of the spirit more than of the flesh. Then, and then only, shall we witness really good and great architecture, really good carpentry, and really good work of any kind.

*From T Raffles Davison (editor),* The Arts connected with Building: Lectures on craftsmanship and design, *delivered at Carpenter's Hall, London Wall, for the Worshipful Company of Carpenters by RW Schultz, CFA Voysey, E Guy Dawber, Laurence A Turner, A Romney Green, MH Baillie Scott, Chas Spooner and J Starkie Gardner, London, 1909.*

TABLEWARE AND OTHER WORK IN SILVER, c1907

CFA VOYSEY AS A YOUNG MAN

# INDIVIDUALITY

## *CFA VOYSEY*

### The Creative Spirit

I have written these chapters in the earnest hope of encouraging my fellow-men to believe and feel the creative spirit within everyone, which while stimulating thought, leads on to mutual sympathy and true union. And so through the working of natural laws, we come to create that beauty which draws us onward and upward.

### A Beneficent and Omnipotent Controlling Power

Let us assume there is a beneficent and omnipotent controlling power, that is perfectly good and perfectly loving; and that our existence here, is for the purpose of growing individual characters. These are the propositions upon which all the following conclusions are based, and the fertile soil out of which our thoughts must grow. This basis of order, and singleness of purpose, will affect our outlook upon nature, and what we make of her must always primarily depend on our attitude of mind towards her.

### There is no Finality to Human Thought – Extension is its Law

The idea of extension is one of the mightiest powers with which we are endowed. However right we are, there remains the idea that we might be more so; there is no finality to human thought – extension is its law. But it seems, human extension and development takes place in alternating spiritual and material directions; as when we sleep for a period, while our bodies being freed from our minds recover those forces that in our waking hours, are the handmaids of our thoughts and feelings. Thus a generation or so is devoted to material needs, and brings forth the engine and the motor and machines in all their manifold forms, making even man into a machine until he shall awaken to a more spiritual activity, and rising above the strengthened forces of his material nature he shall rejoice in a fuller manhood. Surely it is true that war arouses the nobler side of our nature while material prosperity drags us down to the more animal state. So, too, human suffering of all kinds has a softening and mellowing effect and stimulates the growth of all our virtues. Pain produces endeavour, and sorrow brings wisdom. Physical suffering is the parent of pity. We are driven by disease to discover the everlasting laws of nature. And suffering kindles our sympathy for the sorrowful and wages war against selfishness. Dissatisfaction must precede all reform. And so we must overcome evil with good.

As all reforms are first born in one mind, it must be from individual thought and feeling that progress flows. We know that restlessness and discontent are signs of movement. We are advancing most when discontented with ourselves. And we are in that way driven to look for life's essentials, the stable forces of nature, and the most permanent qualities, in order that our building, whatever it may be, may endure. What then are these essentials if not the moral sentiments, spiritual ideas or thoughts having a reality more real than matter; as for instance, reverence, love, justice, mercy, honesty, candour, generosity, humility, loyalty, order, and dignity. These are the real objects of virtue and the common bonds of union between all men in all times and in all places.

Our minds expand with the contemplation of matters of universal interest, and fundamental ideas of lasting importance, while we are narrowed and checked in our sympathy by microscopic enquiry into personal taste and minor details of daily life, although be it remembered, the details of our daily life are the means by which in great measure, the emotions can be aroused and cultivated, depending as they do on our faculty of comparison for their right effect and application. All questions must be brought before the bar of our reason; and each man must assess their relative values according to his temperament, heredity and tradition – hence our differences and therefore our dependence one on another.

If we all had the same affections in like degree, there would be no exchange of ideas, no progress, and dependence and reliance upon each other would be impossible. Dependence kindles love between man and man – independence tends to stifle it. Difference involves friction, and friction involves heat, and heat is force.

A world without individual differences of mind and body is unthinkable.

Yet paradoxical as it may seem, we unite in the reverence and love we cherish for the moral sentiments, because in their varied degrees there is a common basis. It is therefore upon these faculties that individuality must be built.

### Intellectual and Spiritual Culture

Intellectual culture is far more dependent on social and material conditions than is spiritual culture, and so we find individuality cannot be expressed by mere knowledge of affairs, but must rely mainly on moral sentiments and the exercise of reason, in order to establish personality. Hence we find no two minds will record the same facts in exactly the same manner: though making use of the same emotions they will differ in degree. Degrees of intellectual and spiritual culture have always existed, and mark the differences between men far more deeply and truly than any physical differences can do. Seldom do we find the mind and spirit in the same person on equal planes of development.

The scientific mind is often so absorbed with material facts that reason is allowed to slumber. Logical conclusions quite clear to the spiritually active mind, are lost on the materialistic investigator of matter. His conventional methods of enquiry are inapplicable to a spiritual outlook. Theologians will say science is against religion, but no truth can be harmful to any other truth. What is vital and true in the material world must harmonise and agree with all that is vital and true in the spiritual world. Each individual can, if he will, reason in both spheres and find agreement in all vital principles. It is collectivist dogmas and established formulas about which men fight. If the author of matter and spirit be all-powerful and all-good, it is strictly logical to say the verities in the material sphere must harmonise with those in the spiritual, and that no good mind would allow evil to exist except for a good purpose if it were all-powerful. We may conceive of evil being the result of man's misuse of his powers, and being in a state of development he must be imperfect, and his imperfection is to him evil, but to the Creator it may be a necessary part of His gift to us of free will. And therefore a good in disguise. For by our blunders and mistakes we learn all virtues. No virtue could be known but for preceding sin, no light without darkness. And so in our struggle for sincerity against popular conventions we strengthen individuality. Each man who desires to have a clear mind of his own must think all these questions out for

EARLY PHOTOGRAPH OF CFA VOYSEY AND HIS WIFE, MARY MARIA EVANS

himself; they cannot be settled by collective action. And it is a mercy it is so, for our personal views are of infinite importance in the moulding of character.

## The Tyranny of Style

Circumstances often change without changing the mode of expression, whereby the latter loses its quality of fitness. In days of mail, a coat of arms denoted the manner of man that wore it. The loss of fitness, to those who regard the law of fitness as divine, is a blemish and a violation of the sense of reverence. We see innumerable architectural features made use of, long after the circumstances that gave them birth have ceased to exist. Forms and symbols are retained, on sentimental grounds, and because of their associations, long after their meaning has been forgotten.

There are two very distinct types of mind that we must recognise in this connection. The one is mistrustful of self, and must have precedent or authority of some sort to lean upon, even though it be only blind custom. Persons of this type *must* have crutches. They are mostly conformists, and lovers of law and order. The other type is more independent, and enquires into the why and the wherefore, and will be found ready to change the mode to meet changed or changing conditions. These are the non-conformists, who tend most to individuality. They also may love order if they have reverence. The former type tends inevitably to collectivism. Conformity is the very essence of collectivism, as we can still see in the influence of Rome on our conduct in every-day affairs.

There are large bodies of men banded together, not for the improvement of character or the encouragement of individuality, but for the coercion of the multitude into preconceived modes and manners. A cry is now raised for a certain style of architecture, which happens to be at the moment what is called 'the English Renaissance', a style which was first introduced into this country at one of the most morally corrupt periods of the nation's history.

The wealthy had travelled and seen the beauties of foreign countries, and impressions received by them in their moral darkness were all of a materialistic nature. While appreciating the modes of foreign work, they were forgetful of the conditions of climate and national character, and expressions of emotion were not what they looked for, and love of truth was neglected. There were cultured architects of exquisite taste, like Sir Christopher Wren, who showed his fine sense of proportion, in the foreign tongue. He, no doubt, was quite conscious that the accentuation of jointing of stone-work, known as rustication, was originally a deliberate attempt to deceive, it being adopted to make walls look more solid than they really were, a direct and immoral effort on the part of the originators, who were quite prolific in that form of falsehood, and possibly like their imitators of today, were quite unconscious they were doing anything wrong.

It is inconceivable that so many of our leading architects at the present time should be reviving these samples of ancient sin, and, at the same time, believe them to be evil. Collectivism and conformity have made them mimic the manners of those they looked up to; sincerity and honesty of expression has been dominated by fashion, and forms are now used for their material qualities only, regardless of their spiritual significance.

The return to the forms and modes of a corrupt period indicates that modes have lost their moral significance, and that men have become so materialistic that they cannot discern more than material qualities, so that buildings to them are nothing more than combinations of form, colour, texture, light and shade. Moral qualities are smothered by the parasite of materialism which has twined its tendrils about every branch.

How powerful conventions may become it is easy to see. A style accepted by general consent is of the essence of a tyrant. Symmetry, for instance, will impose its iron law, and lead the architect to cover his library door with books, if the door by proclaiming itself should upset the symmetrical balance of the room; surely that which requires fraud to defend it cannot be morally sound.

Multitudes of examples could be mentioned where candour, truth, and fitness are sacrificed to conformity to so-called style.

## Collectivism

It is the universal law that whatever pursuit, whatever doctrine becomes fashionable, shall lose a portion of that dignity, which it had possessed while it was confined to a small but earnest minority, and was loved for its own sake alone. (Macaulay)

Collectivism, convention and fashion all derive their power through the suppression of the individual. Men's minds and bodies are forced into grooves and moulded into machine-like order; being banded together like soldiers for a common purpose, their united efforts gather accumulating strength.

Collectivism must then be judged by the aim in view, and cannot be regarded as a general principal to be lightly adopted. Like all physical force, it will work for good or ill with equal facility; thus only when we know the aim is good, can we uphold the system. Individuality being the basis of character, collectivism can have but little effect that is not harmful to its development. Conduct can be controlled by collective action, but conduct is not character, nor is it always the result of character. Collectivism is a form of compulsion that cannot have the same ethical value and effect on character that individual free choice must always have. It requires but little effort to swim with the stream, and slide almost unconsciously into the modes and manners of the multitude. We become easily satisfied with a standard more or less defined and established in the mind, whereas the individualist's standard is ever evolving towards a greater perfection.

Many speak and act as if multitudes of men were incapable of self-culture and that therefore collectivism is necessary, and clearly defined lines of action must be imposed upon them. But against definite restriction to individual liberty men have fought in all times. And yet it is not quite possible to agree, that Government should confine its forces to the protection of the weak against the strong, leaving every man to work out his own salvation in the domain of thought and feeling?

We have no right to assume that large masses of men are depraved, or incapable of self-culture. The idea has given rise to all manner of laws that degrade rather than elevate. Moral sentiments are not always recognised as universal, and hence it is we tyrannise over one another. It would seem that if every man is blessed with the same fundamental sentiments, and our differences are only those of degree, much more can be accomplished by persuasion than by force, and by taking for granted that every man has the feeling we should desire to cultivate. If then liberty of thought is essential to the growth of character, combined coercion of any kind which limits thought must check its development. Furthermore, the great danger of collectivist action is in the acceptance of a given idea as final, and fixed in its value; silencing the individual conscience and discouraging personal criticism and enquiry. It also presents a beaten track to the idle traveller who shirks the strain of a rugged way.

Conduct controlled by custom petrifies intelligent reasoning and creative enterprise, and leads us to act like machines with the inevitable neglect of all aesthetic thought. All personal feeling is suppressed, and sincerity is not called upon; therefore Collectivism must enslave, and while killing individuality makes men more materialistic. It also accentuates class differences and encourages prejudice, hence sects are multiplied and contentions ensue. Theories are tried by cliques, and often become discredited by their power to attract the thoughtless and superficial. For example, garden suburb societies spring into being, and gather a certain class of mind that responds to the principle theory of the society, but in

CFA VOYSEY AT THE DOOR OF 'THE ORCHARD', CHORLEY WOOD

time the union becomes limited by the exhaustion of energy. Great reforms are expected when two or three are gathered together, but disappointment invariably follows.

The fascination of having our thinking done for us is very real to minds already jaded by materialistic interests, and so the needs of the flesh will jostle out the thoughts of the spirit. Thus we find collectivism powerful in relieving us from personal responsibility and anxiety. We require little mental effort in obeying established habits, and after a time become automatic in thought and action. It is a kind of lathe process that turns off all individual knots and angles, and smooths us all down to one standard pattern.

It is difficult to persuade others that pain is a blessing in disguise, that the struggle that strains is strengthening, that to enquire of oneself the why and the wherefore of all our likes and dislikes is immensely helpful, and stimulating to reason and justice. Creative artists must go through this process of reason, if they would avoid becoming slaves to pure innovation and the prey of fashion mongers. Many architects of today say in effect, 'let us have an established mode, a national style of architecture. Save us from the individual, who, if left alone, will shock our prejudices, and violate our established ideas. The standard of past ages is good enough for us and must be kept up, even at the sacrifice of buildings have been produced during the last generation or so, is deeply degrading to the individuals who compete; instead of evolving the character of each edifice out of requirements, and conditions, moulded in sincerity with hearts set on moral sentiments; the mode or style thought to be favoured by the authorities is assumed and set up as the keynote of requirements and conditions must be tuned. The design, instead of proceeding from within outwards, is forced from without inwards. Colonnades and cornices that have done duty for temples, town halls, and theatres, or clothed our public baths, banks and Baptist chapels, crop up everywhere, being compressed or extended to fit the size required. This standardising is, no doubt, good for the immediate profits of trade, but it will not make men mentally or spiritually better. The system that crushes individual sincerity cannot bring lasting credit to any community.

### Modes Helpful to the Expression of Individuality
Gothic architecture grew out of the careful consideration of requirements and conditions, and obedience to the natural qualities of materials; in fact, all the best building throughout the world has grown in that way, and was ever so created, until men became corrupted by materialistic ideas, and then the mode of expression was regarded as more important than the conditions and requirements with which they were dealing. The fascination of the mode of a Grecian Temple led to the endeavour to adapt it to a mansion house. Individual grappling with conditions and requirements by men of lofty moral sense, has given us the finest and purest architecture. A reverence for climatic and other natural national conditions spiritual, as well as material, has produced in this country its glorious cathedrals, colleges and Tudor houses.

Could we but revive the individualistic spirit and stimulate moral sentiments, then, we should once more have a noble national architecture, without any revival of any particular style, either native or foreign. Certain conventions, dictated by a complete knowledge of material and needs, would naturally lead to the use of many familiar forms. The principles of the lintel and the arch, which are based on material qualities, must for ever remain true principles. But if we cast behind us all preconceived styles, our work will still possess a style, but it will be a living natural and true expression of modern needs and ideals: not an insincere imitation of other nations or other times.

The tyranny of imposing a mode of expression in any of the arts must seriously check individual sincerity and lead to an indifference to truth, which is the most corrupting of influences.

Men cannot be honest while imitating sentiments which they often neither feel or understand. It is because we are not sincere in our building, not aiming at individuality, but are dominated by collectivism, that our Public Buildings are so dumb and death-like; many have the qualities of good proportion, clever, ingenious construction, sensible use of material, and such like charms, but for the expression of living sentiment and spiritual force – such as our old houses and cathedrals present – they are silent, dead, soulless piles of mortifying insincerity, which only sadden us.

The lack of noble sentiment in our modern buildings is due to the materialism of the age, which has led to the assumption of a foreign style, and the acquisition of material qualities only. Thought and feeling are ignored, hence the works are still-born. Individuality is not called for, but conformity to old conventions and standard modes are imposed by collective opinion. We are not allowed to work out our own salvation, but must tread the road that is easiest for the duffer. Democracy, as it becomes more articulate and better organised, becomes more mechanical, and less able or willing to recognise individuality. Convention relieves the individual from thought and anxiety. We say 'there is safety in numbers', and that in a multitude of councillors there is great wisdom. But this false philosophy is itself the outcome of fear, and must be uprooted before we shall acquire true independence and manly courage.

Our domestic architecture has advanced much more than that of our public buildings, because we have cast off the tyranny of styles, and refused to be hampered by any preconceived mode. While devoting the whole mind to meeting most fitly, all the existing requirements and conditions; on the other hand, unfortunately, materialism has led to the consideration of material fitness only. For their homes many people say, 'Give us personal ease and comfort – we do not want sentiment.' The styles as taught in the schools have been gradually discredited in the search for greater fitness, and the process was greatly accelerated by the introduction of machinery, which has revolutionised our methods of production, construction and design.

Of course, we look not for dignity in the front door while struggling to make it look better than it is. If it is not oak, must it not be painted to look like it? Were individual conscientiousness more appreciated, the artist would be allowed greater freedom, instead of as now being treated as a tradesman and paid hireling, who's duty it is only to carry out instructions and make good bargains.

While artists are alive to all practical considerations, and are ready to meet all requirements and conditions imposed upon them, recognising such as the best foundations for design, there is still left a wide field in which the emotions can, and should, operate to the mutual advantage of all. It is only blindness to these qualities that has led to the servility of art workers. To save his pocket he has often to lose his soul. Frankness is not to his worldly advantage. It has not always been so, nor can it for long remain. Our spirits must have an awakening, and we must see that the imposition of any style, dictates a mode of expression false and foreign to the designer, and the employment of forms, originally intended to deceive the eye, violates the conscience and vitiates the taste.

It has often been observed that the architecture of a people, must always be a true reflection of their moral and spiritual condition. And in an age where you find a prolific display of deceptions, you may be sure that the people are more materially than spiritually advanced, and more collectivist than individual.

In early Tudor times the aristocratic idea was more alive than it is today, and there was in consequence much patronage of individuals. Moral sentiments were then as fashionable as motor cars are now.

Another mode helpful to the growth of individuality, and all its attendant blessings, would be the removal of all doctrinal restrictions from men when in the pulpit. But we must not pursue this thorny subject, as many will think the mere mention of it is enough to condemn individuality altogether. Nevertheless our zeal for freedom of thought grows out of a reverence for truth and faithfulness; and, while the cultivation of ethics must involve the recognition of law and order, loyalty is only possible to the free mind. Obedience you may have from the slave, but loyalty a man can only bestow freely, and it is an addition to, not a part of, his obedience.

Many are the channels though which the ship of personality may navigate, and multiform the winds of emotion that blow hither and thither, safety only being possible while one mind holds the helm. You may lead and encourage the Captain by kindness, which cannot weaken responsibility, but never must external authority usurp the throne. We must see more and more clearly the difference between obedience to an inner monitor and conformity to outside pressure, whether proceeding from one or many, and this perception will make us recoil more and more from collectivism.

The study of dress is very illuminating to this question of individuality. Instinctively we feel the outward semblance of equality as conducive to social intercourse, hence the fashion for dressing all men like waiters when they are to dine together. The desire to hide material differences is the underlying principle of all uniforms. It is the same for large bodies of men required to express unity of purpose. The Military and Naval uniforms enhance the effect of terror and apparent power of an enemy. It is a splendid institution even for bank clerks, or Stock Exchange men. There can be no harm in having them labelled with silk hats. But there is yet a fascination in perceiving the difference of vocation in differences of dress; and the more attention the individual gives to his own costume, the more enlightening it becomes. He cannot disguise his temperament or help telling you if his sympathies are more with a period in history than with the grace of Nature. He will conform or not to the fashions of those he respects, according to the power of his own sentiments. A natural shyness, and desire not to attract attention, will lead him to suppress his personal feeling almost to extinction. More powerful still is the inclination felt by the individualist, to differentiate; fashions will be avoided by him which he finds favoured by those socially beneath him. This is a natural instinct often found operating quite unconsciously.

The point most worthy of attention, however, is not a question as to the relative values of uniformity or variety; but an enquiry as to how to influence the development of any costume, so as to make it a benefit to personal character. At present it seems mainly governed by commercial considerations.

If, however, dress is to be regarded as a means of culture, as well as a protection, and an affair of commerce from the production of which millions get their living, moral sentiments will have to be acknowledged and taken into account much more than they are at present. Reverence, truth, honesty, candour, generosity, humility, order, and directness will have to dominate and suppress the collective energy of change-mongers. Human machines for stimulating human wants are very good for trade, and help men to amass wealth. If wealth is our sole aim, there is no more to be said; but if our aim is the cultivation of character, greater individuality will conduce to greater sincerity; and any dislocation of trade that might follow from the suppression of collectivism, would be amply compensated by the general culture accruing. It cannot be doubted that, but for fashion, men and women would take keener delight in beautifying costume. Interest in the grace and loveliness of forms, colours and textures of everyday life must work magic on our characters, and send into oblivion much of our sordid materialism. Change the motive for our dressing, from competitive rivalry into an act of reverence towards the body, expressive of the higher qualities of mind, and you then convert costume into a means of culture and minister of beauty. Individualism, then, is the main cure for the present ugliness of dress, and the more we tend to follow fashion, the more collectivist we shall become; and by aiding the commercial instinct in the tradesman, we starve to death those sentiments we all value, and would gladly encourage.

Recognition in the mind of individuals, of the moral significance of all humanly created things, is all we ask for. It ought not to be necessary to write or speak about such a matter. It is so powerful a force that one marvels that is so commonly neglected and so often absent from the mind altogether. The spirit of man requires nourishment as much as his body; and yet how content many of us are to starve our spiritual nature, and cultivate a calm endurance of the ugliness around us.

It is interesting to note how some modern scientists are beginning to show a restless discontent with materialism pure and simple, and are seeking to articulate the divine impulse of the spirit.

We long to see it demonstrated and accepted by all men that the spirit behind all matter is more loveable than matter itself; and, while it cannot be handed from one to another, it is not to be possessed by all. Through individual thought and feeling we shall see, and create, what collectively we can only defile.

## Love, Justice, Mercy and Generosity

Love, justice, mercy, and generosity are qualities that must be felt by those who would seek them in the works of man – each and all may chant songs of praise in stone as much as in a story. Our buildings, our books, and our furniture cry out at us for shame! When greed has ground down every worker and drowned justice and mercy beneath its arrogant elaboration.

The sacrifice of enrichment and display, or even accommodation in order to gain greater perfection in secret places, and care for servants instead of costly carvings, are the directions in which much can be done to establish the character of generosity.

Concentrated ornament will help us towards making that ornament finer and more effective, as well as assisting towards the improvement in the quality generally. The building covered with indifferent decoration invariably exhibits a sacrifice of general quality. Structural parts are cheapened to pay for gaudy display. A sense of order which precedes and follows from punctuality and precision, and inspires faith, can be conveyed even in the arrangement of a tradesman's notice. One simple type instead of many will show a steadiness that reminds us of a reliable man, it is orderly and controlled, simple and frank, not decked out with flourishes and formed with variegated proportions. Why, if we have any information to convey, should we seek to dazzle the eye and satiate the brain? Like the modern shopkeeper, who thinks he can charm the buyer by showing all the wares at once.

Material matters have developed at such a pace it is hard to avoid being swept along with the tide. To be mindful of more than the needs of the flesh when shopping, is most difficult to the average mortal; so much is studiously prepared to intoxicate and bewilder the higher instincts. The sense of beauty which is common to all is carefully poisoned at the fountain head by our early training in modes. Our knapsack of knowledge has one small compartment into which certain examples of the beautiful are placed, and these we take out on our travels and compare with what we meet in order to formulate our judgement. The process is like the mechanical stonecrusher, it destroys the heart in every thing that falls beneath its weight. We have thus grown to rely on museums as essential for the poor who cannot travel.

With what result? Is the peasant work of today to be compared for spiritual beauty with the work of the 13th and 14th centuries? It is not the experience of travel that quickens the spirit, but experience of thought and feeling. We have relied too much and too long on material things. Museums full of unused articles divorced from the purpose of their being, are like mausoleums. Oh! departed voices, still audible to the sympathetic spirit, what intense joy might we not feel, if we could but thrill with the sentiments that gave you birth, and drink beneath the substance of your being until we are intoxicated with the same emotions.

We must be generously disposed before we can impart to matter that quality which will keep it alive in our affections. The beam must look strong enough for its task as well as be so. The thin, skinny mullions with cottonlike lead glazing suggest only meanness. Generosity can only show in our work when we are forgetful of our own gain, and bursting to bestow the best that is in us, and glory in straining every nerve towards perfect feeling and fitting expression. The generous love of beauty will prompt attention to the meanest detail. To the generous mind no detail is too small, or too insignificant to be worthy of our efforts to make it beautiful. The bestowal of grace is a devotion as much when manifested in the kitchen as in the cathedral.

## On the War of 1914-18

Surely it is evident that the most far-reaching and important effect of the present war, will be to force men to distinguish more clearly between intellectual and spiritual culture, and thus to encourage the latter and by so doing strengthen and sustain individuality.

*CFA Voysey,* Individuality, *Chapman & Hall, London, 1915.*

PORTRAIT OF CFA VOYSEY BY HAROLD SPEED

NEW PLACE, 1897

# ON CONCRETE
## THE ARCHITECT AND ENGINEER

. . . Concrete in itself is an ugly thing. But concrete construction considered as a servant and as means to an end can be made a ministering angel. It is a good servant, but a bad master. A good servant only so long as it is kept in its place. There are many kinds of buildings which, it could be argued, would be more suitably constructed in concrete than in any other material. But there are others for which concrete would be most unsuited. It is therefore necessary to admit the unique character of concrete in order to use it fittingly and artistically.

The choice of our material, when designing a building, is like the choice of words and phrases when we are writing or speaking. It is never an affair of the pocket only. The pounds, shilling and pence argument must not be permitted to spread its poisoned gases all over aesthetic considerations, that is, if the world is to be made better.

We shall surely all agree that proportion is of vital importance to the subject in hand. The sense of relation is only another aspect of the sense of proportion. It enters into all the affairs of life and into our calculations of fitness. It is the manifestation of personal character.

It is my firm conviction that the beauty of concrete construction must consist in right proportions. What are right proportions? Each must ask and answer for himself. I refuse to have any formula forced upon me, either Greek, Roman or Gothic. It is a matter of feeling and is capable of refinement, for ever evolving and developing as we advance in spiritual, moral and intellectual culture. We want no dogmatic statements of what is good proportion any more than we need a definition of truth and beauty. All are growths, for ever being purified and lifted higher.

It is quite true that the Greeks arrived at what we regard as perfect proportion, but it was perfection as applied to given objects. Definite groups of requirements and conditions were beautifully proportioned, but to copy these proportions in designing the portico of a new public house is like grasping at the shadow and forgetting the substance. It is like using Latin quotations to an audience of peasants; it serves well to glorify the speaker and suggest his superiority. But oh! what a contemptible vanity it is!

There is one thing for which we must be thankful to concrete construction, namely, that it has forced upon us the necessity for a revision of the building bylaws. These foolish and mischievous irritations must be revised, if not repealed altogether, for the stupidity of veneering concrete construction so as to give it the appearance of stone is fraudulent as well as foolish. Veneer, when frankly applied, is legitimate enough, but it is open to question as to whether a concrete building cannot be made beautiful and satisfying without veneering it all over. The texture of concrete might be made as pleasant as stucco. It is quite doubtful whether we should allow the expenditure on veneer, the purpose of which is purely and only to enhance appearances. True architectural beauty, to my mind, must be wedded to structural function. Therefore the form of your concrete and mode of its use must embody elements of beauty, and not depend for its charm entirely on superimposed material of quite another nature. This suggestion can only be applied in certain cases, and is not a principle of general application. It should not be used as an argument against mural painting or mosaic. It would surely be quite possible to put up concrete buildings in good proportions with the concrete walls exposed to view in naked frankness and wedded to certain features of stone or native marble. The main entrance of such a building, gilded, would surely be quite legitimate treatment.

The most difficult branch of this subject would seem to be suggested by the question: how far may we, for the sake of calling up association of ideas, use the arch form?

We cannot deny that the Gothic arch has a profound effect on our minds and hearts, and is structurally the practical outcome of small stones and bricks. The lintel would seem, structurally speaking, the most suitable form for concrete construction. The four-centred arch of Tudor times can be made in concrete, but it is surely more complex than the lintel. The slightly pointed arch is so dear to me that I want to modify and limit all my principles to admit to it. Like all weaklings, I wish to be sound and logical, but pure feeling, which enemies sneer at and call sentiment, gets possession of me and carries me off into the clouds. We love to appear intellectually great and scientifically sound, but not at the expense of all human emotion. This little touch of inconsistency, this human frailty that abandons itself to pure emotion is one of the most human of all human charms, and thus it comes about that it is the unseen that is the glory of the seen. The emotion is buried beneath matter, not to rot, but to regenerate.

*This is an extract from 'The Aesthetic Aspects of Concrete Construction', The Architect and Engineer, Vol 57, May 1919.*

# CHRONOLOGY

Reference is made here only to selected buildings. For fuller details on Voysey's architectural works see individual project descriptions, 'Selected Surviving Buildings' and 'Selected Unexecuted Projects'.

## 1857
Born on 28 May at Hessle in Yorkshire, CFA Voysey was the eldest of Frances and Reverend Charles Voysey's ten children.

Voysey's grandfather, Annesley Voysey (1794-1834), was a successful architect. Despite family connections with John Wesley, Voysey's father had been ordained into the Church of England in 1852. He served as a curate in several parishes including those in Hessle, Craigton in Jamaica, Great Yarmouth, Whitechapel and Victoria Docks.

## 1864
Rev Charles Voysey was appointed vicar of Healaugh, a small parish, outside York.

## 1869
When Reverend Charles Voysey was summoned to appear before the Chancellor's Court of the Diocese of York, as a consequence of his unorthodox preaching and publications, the verdict went against him.

## 1871
The Reverend Voysey was 'deprived of his living' as the decision of the York Chancellor was upheld by the Privy Chancellor. He, however, continued to hold church services and presently established the Theistic Church.

## 1872
Voysey attended Dulwich College for 18 months. After this JCL Sparkes, the school's progressive art master, became his private tutor.

## 1873
He was articled to John Pollard Seddon (1827-1906), the Gothic Revivalist architect. Voysey's first professional experience was of working on country churches. It is probable that he learned the art of decorative design from Seddon as the practice produced designs for tile manufacturers.

## 1877
Voysey started taking on his own commissions such as minor house alterations and surveys.

## 1879
The depression led to a dearth of work in Seddon's office. Having completed his articles, Voysey went to work for Henry Saxon Snell (1830-1904), who specialised in the design of hospitals and charitable institutions.

## 1880
Voysey joined the office of George Devey (1820-1886), the country house architect, as an 'improver'. The introduction, in all probability, came through the elder Voysey since Devey was an active member of the Theistic Church.

## 1881
Voysey set up his own practice in Queen Anne's Gate and later in Broadway chambers, Westminster. He designed a large sanatorium at Teignmouth, Devon, but it was never realised. He also entered a competition for the Admiralty offices in Whitehall; his entry was not placed.

## 1883
At the suggestion of the architect AH Mackmurdo (1851-1942), Voysey began to design wallpapers and textiles. Initially he sold designs to Jeffrey & Co.

## 1884
Voysey joined the Art Workers Guild, whose earliest members had been the leading Arts and Crafts activists of the day.

## 1885
In July, Voysey married Mary Maria Evans; their first home was in Bedford Park but they soon moved to Streatham Hill. He drew up designs for a buttressed half-timbered house, supposedly for himself and his wife, and a 'house with an octagonal hall'.

## 1888-89
Voysey designed his first built work, The Cottage in Bishop's Itchington, near Warwick, for MHJ Lakin.

## 1890-91
Voysey moved to St John's Wood. Although an area favoured by artists and intellectuals, his new address was also one indicative of success.

## 1891
JW Forster commissioned Voysey to design him a house in Bedford Park.

## 1891-92
Voysey designed his only real town-houses in Hans Road, off the Brompton Road, South Kensington.

## 1893
*The Studio*, which was to be instrumental in promoting both Voysey and the achievements of the Arts and Crafts Movement, was launched in April. Voysey illustrated the cover.

## 1894
Voysey designed Lowicks, near Frensham, in Surrey.

## 1895
Annesley Lodge, Hampstead, was built by Voysey for his father, the Reverend Charles Voysey.

## 1896
Greyfriars, near Guildford, in Surrey, was designed for the American-born writer Julian Russell Sturgis (1848-1904).

## 1897
The publisher, AMM Stedman, commissioned Voysey to build New Place, Haslemere.

**1898**

Voysey designed Broadleys and Moorcrag, near Lake Windermere.

**1899**

Voysey started drawing up plans for The Orchard, his own home in Chorley Wood, Hertfordshire. He set up his office in Baker Street, near Marylebone Station, within easy commuting distance.

He designed the Spade House for HG Wells.

**1902**

A Sanderson & Sons, to whom Voysey had regularly supplied wallpaper designs, commissioned him to build a factory in Chiswick.

**1909**

*Ideas in Things* was published.

**1914**

The outbreak of the War marked the end of Voysey's architectural career. He continued to produce designs for wallpapers, textiles and carpets.

**1915**

*Individuality* was published as one of two lectures.

**1917**

Voysey moved to a flat in St James' Street, off Piccadilly, where he was to live and work until a few months before his death.

**1918**

In a letter to his friend Alexander Morton, the Carlisle textile manufacturer, Voysey wrote of his 'terrible plight' financially and asked for work.

**1919-20**

Designs were produced by Voysey for war memorials at Malvern Wells and Potter's Bar, Hertfordshire.

**1924**

Voysey was elected Master of the Art Workers' Guild.

**1927**

A series of articles on Voysey were published in *The Architect and Building News*.

**1931**

An exhibition of Voysey's work was held at the Batsford Gallery under the auspices of *Architectural Review*. In the same journal John Betjeman devoted an article to him.

**1934**

Voysey was cited as a precursor of the new architecture by the architect Raymond McGrath in *Twentieth Century Houses*.

**1936**

The distinction of Designer for Industry was awarded to Voysey by the Royal Society of Arts.

**1940**

Voysey was awarded the Gold Medal of the Royal Institute of British Architects, its highest honour.

His son Cowles Voysey, the architect, took him to live in Winchester, to escape the blitz in London.

**1941**

Voysey died on 12 February, in Winchester.

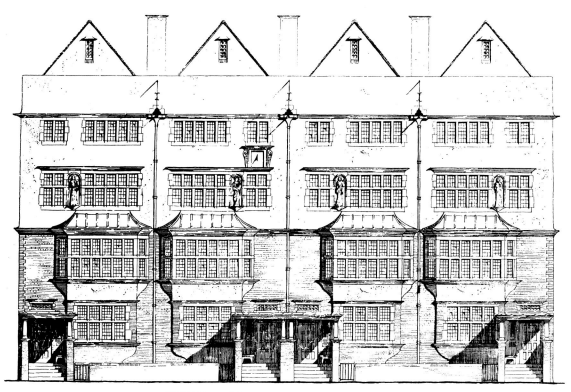

UNEXECUTED DESIGN FOR HOUSES, SWAN WALK, CHELSEA, 1891

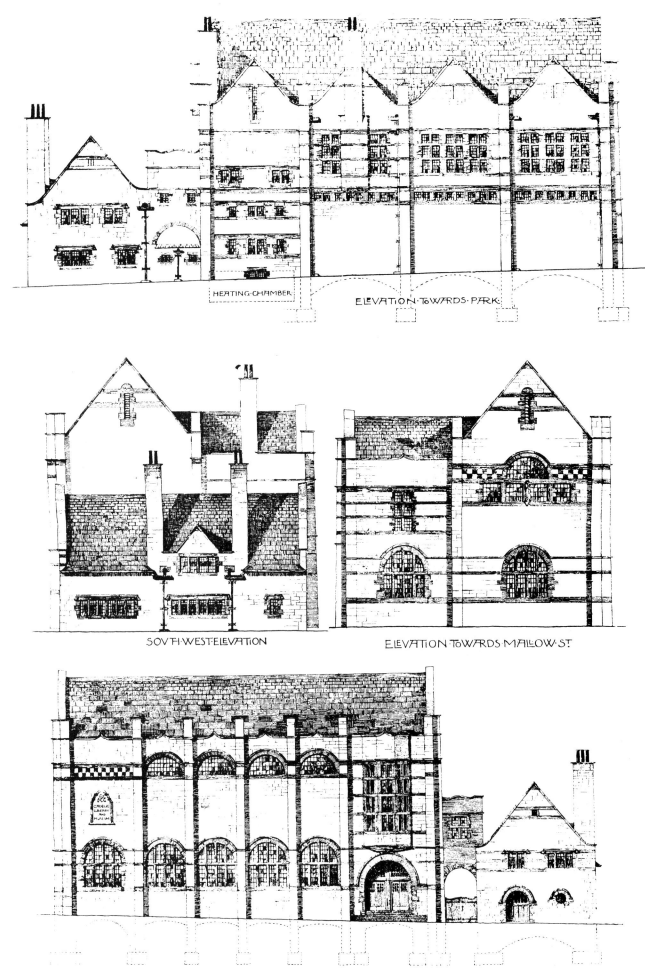

HEATING·CHAMBER

ELEVATION·TOWARDS·PARK·

SOUTH·WEST·ELEVATION

ELEVATION·TOWARDS·MALLOW·ST

UNEXECUTED ELEVATIONS OF THE CARNEGIE LIBRARY AND MUSEUM, LIMERICK, IRELAND, c1904

# SELECTED UNEXECUTED PROJECTS

**1882-84**

Competition entry for Admiralty Buildings in Whitehall: no record of this project appears to have survived.

Sanatorium for the Teignmouth Sanatorium Company, Devonshire: a drawing of the principal elevation was published in *Dekorative Kunst*, I, Munich, 1897.

Design for crematorium in Ayr, Scotland.

**c1885**

Voysey's own cottage: the designs were published in *The Studio*, IV, 1894 and *Dekorative Kunst*, I, Munich, 1897, in a modified version.

Design for a house with an octagonal hall: published in *The British Architect*, XXXI, 1889 and *Dekorative Kunst*, I, 1897.

The house with a hall is so different, in stylistic terms, from the cottage that it is inconceivable that it is not the later design. The influence of George Devey, and to some extent Norman Shaw, is apparent in this work.

**1888**

Design for a house at Bedford Park, Chiswick, for Mrs Forster: the drawings are in The Drawings Collection, RIBA. A modified version of this was built in 1891 (see 14 South Parade).

**1889**

Design for 'a tower house': published in *The British Architect*, XXXI, 1889. Voysey was to return to the same theme in 1903.

**1891**

Speculative terrace houses at Swan Walk, off Chelsea Embankment, for Daw & Sons.

**1892**

Studio in Glebe Place, Chelsea, for Conrad Dressler. (Dressler was a well-known Arts and Crafts ceramicist.)

**1894-95**

Designs for a large house, at Ockham, Surrey, for the Earl of Lovelace: published in *The British Architect*, XLIV, 1895.

**1895**

First project for studios at Studland Bay, Swanage, Dorset, for A Sutro: a modified scheme was executed in 1896.

**1897**

Design for Dixcot, North Drive, Tooting Bec Common: this was commissioned by RW Essex, for whom Voysey designed many wallpapers. The house was to be built, but under the superintendence of Walter Cave, a prominent Arts and Crafts architect.

**1897-1903**

Designs for houses at: Thorpe Mandeville, Northamptonshire; Limpsfield, Surrey; Ashbourne, Derbyshire; Oxshott, Surrey; Colnebrook, Middlesex; Malvern, Hereford and Worcester; Haslemere, Surrey; Hampstead, London; and Kirkoswald, Lake Windermere.

**c1901**

Designs for Lincoln Grammar School: published in *The Building News*, LXXVI, 1905. The school was built to the design of an Arts and Crafts architect, Leonard Stokes.

**1903**

Design for 'a tower house' at Bognor, Sussex, for W Ward Higgs: published in *Moderne Bauformen*, IV, Stuttgart, 1905.

**c1904**

Competition design for the Carnegie Library and Museum, Limerick, Ireland: illustrated in *The British Architect*, LXIV, 1905.

**1904-08**

Designs for houses at: Alderley Edge, Cheshire; Chorley Wood, Hertfordshire; Stoke Poges, Buckinghamshire; Blackburn, Lancashire; Chorley, Lancashire; Frinton-on-Sea, Essex; Knotty Green, Beaconsfield, Buckinghamshire.

**1910**

Two office blocks in Tudor Street, London, EC4, for the Spicer Brothers.

**1912**

Shop at 145 Victoria Street, London, SW1, for Perry & Company.

**1913**

Small house at Ampthill, Bedfordshire.

**1914**

Competition drawings for Government buildings at Ottawa, Canada: executed in a medievalising style.

Designs for houses at: Wilmslow, Cheshire; Ashmansworth, Tewbury, Berkshire; and Thatcham Coldash, Berkshire.

**1920**

House at Laughton, Market Harborough, Leicestershire.

**1922**

Designs for houses at: Jihlava, Czechoslovakia and St Nicholas-at-Wade, Isle of Thanet, Kent.

**1923**

Design for two tall blocks of flats for the Devonshire House site, Piccadilly: although evidently influenced by North American skyscraper design, the blocks have a markedly medieval aspect.

**1933**

Competition design for a Manchester Exhibition Hall: Voysey's last essay in architecture. The proposed building was in a late medieval style, not unlike his Ottawa Government buildings of 1914. RH Uren won the competition with a modern design.

# SELECTED SURVIVING PROJECTS

See project descriptions for more detailed information on particular buildings.

**1888**
The Cottage, Station Road, Bishop's Itchington, Warwick, for MH Lakin.

**1890**
Walnut Tree Farm, Castlemorton, Hereford and Worcester, for H Cazalet.

**1891**
Studio at 17 St Dunstan's Road, W6 for WEF Britten.
14 South Parade, Bedford Park, Chiswick, W4, for JW Forster.

**1891-92**
14 and 16 Hans Road, London, SW3 for Archibald Grove.

**1893**
Perrycroft, Jubilee Drive, Colwall, near Great Malvern, Hereford and Worcester, for JW Wilson.

**1894**
Lowicks House, Tilford, near Frensham, Surrey, for EJ Horniman.

**1895**
The Wentworth Arms Inn, Elmesthorpe, Hinckley, Leicestershire, commissioned by the Earl of Lovelace. Voysey also designed a large house at Ockham Park, Surrey, for the Earl in 1894-95, which was never built.
    Annesley Lodge, Platts Lane, London, NW3 was designed for the architect's father, the Reverend Charles Voysey.

**1896**
Wortley Cottages, Elmesthorpe, Hinckley, Leicestershire for the Earl of Lovelace: originally thatched, the Cottages are fairly close to vernacular tradition.
    Greyfriars, the Hog's Back, near Guildford, Surrey, for Julian Russell Sturgis.

**1897**
Hill Close, Studland Bay, Swanage, Dorset: originally a studio-house for A Sutro, the buttressing seems excessive for a comparatively small structure. It was illustrated in several contemporary publications. It has been unsympathetically altered in recent times.

**1897**
Norney Grange, near Eashing, Godalming, Surrey, for the Reverend W Leighton Crane.
    The Hill, Thorpe Mandeville, Northamptonshire, for Hope Brooke.
    New Place, Farnham Lane, Haslemere, Surrey, for AAM Stedman.

**1898**
Broadleys, Gillhead, near Cartmel Fell, Lake Windermere, Cumbria, for A Currer Briggs.
    Moorcrag, Gillhead, near Cartmel Fell, Lake Windermere, Cumbria, for JW Buckley.

**1899**
Spade House, Radnor Cliff Crescent, Sandgate, Folkestone, Kent, for HG Wells.
    Winsford Cottage Hospital, Halwill, Devon: this was originally called Beaworthy Cottage Hospital. The additions are not by Voysey. Voysey had no doubt learned the essentials of hospital design from H Saxon Snell (1830-1904) a specialist in this field for whom he worked briefly 1879-80. Voysey's first surviving design on paper was for a sanatorium at Teignmouth, Devon. This ambitious project came to nothing.
    Oakhill, 54 Oakhill Grove Crescent, Kidderminster, Worcestershire, for FJ Mayers.
    The Orchard, Shire Lane, Chorley Wood, Hertfordshire, for Voysey and his family.

**1900**
Prior's Garth, Puttenham, Surrey, for FH Chambers: later additions were by T Muntzer, John Brandon-Jones and Ashton and others. Later called Priorsfield. This is not among the most successful of Voysey's houses. The pitched roofs, steeper than normal for Voysey, do not improve the overall effect.

**1901**
The Pastures, North Luffenham, near Stamford, Leicestershire, for Miss G Conant.

**1902**
Factory for Sanderson & Sons, wallpaper manufacturers, 10 Barley Mow Passage, Chiswick, London W4: some 6000 of the original glazed bricks have recently been refaced with the aid of a grant from English Heritage.
    Voysey's only factory was faced with white glazed bricks of the kind used in light-wells. The idea of cladding an urban building with washable tiles seems to have been first mooted by Viollet-le-Duc in the illustrated Atlas which accompanied his *Entretiens* of 1863-72. The architect Halsey Ricardo, a pupil of Norman Shaw, had also used glazed bricks on houses in Kensington in 1894. The Sanderson factory has certain affinities with large water-mills of the kind found in southern England. One may also detect an affinity with Thomas Telford's St Katharine Docks which were begun in 1802. The buttresses conceal ventilating ducts – Voysey became interested in ventilation while working for Saxon Snell, according to John Brandon-Jones. The curving parapet, which links the buttresses, is a feature which may well have its origins in the exhibition stand which AH Mackmurdo designed for The Century Guild Liverpool exhibition of 1886.
    Vodin, Old Woking Road, Pyrford, Surrey, for F Walters. Now called Little Court.

**1903**
Ty-Bronna, St Fagan's Road, Fairwater, near Cardiff, Glamorgan, for W Hastings Watson: somewhat modified, the house has lost a great deal of its original character.
    White Cottage, 68 Lyford Road, Wandsworth, London, SW18, for CT Coggin: alterations have been made to the original design.

Tilehurst, 10 Grange Road, Bushey, Hertfordshire, for Miss Somers: the large porch is perhaps the house's most notable feature. Littleholme, Kendal, 1909, has a similar though slightly larger porch. Miss Somers ran a small convalescent home for children, which was also designed by Voysey.

Hollybank, Shire Lane, Chorley Wood, Hertfordshire, for Dr HRT Fort. The house is near The Orchard, Voysey's own house.

## 1904

Myholme, Merry Hill Lane, Bushey, Hertfordshire, for Miss Somers: some alterations have been made to the orignal house.

## 1904-05

Miners' institute and houses, Whitwood near Normanton, Yorkshire, for Henry Briggs and Son: precedents for such a housing scheme in Yorkshire included Copley (1800-20), Saltaire (1850s), Ackroydon, Halifax, (1861-63). The overall look of the housing at Whitwood with its alternating pattern of gables and dormers is quite close to the Ackroydon scheme. The Whitwood houses were not built under Voysey's superintendence, but their detailing is entirely characteristic of his work.

## 1905

The White Horse Inn, Stechworth, Cambridgeshire, for the Earl of Ellesmere.

Hollymount, Beaconsfield, Buckinghamshire, for CT Burke.

The Homestead, Second Avenue, Frinton-on-Sea, Essex, for SC Turner.

House at Aswan, Egypt, for Dr Leigh Canney.

## 1906-07

Littleholme, Guildford, Surrey, for G Muntzer.

## 1909

Littleholme, 103 Sedburgh Road, Kendal, Cumbria, for AW Simpson.

A holiday cottage, Slindon, Barnham Junction, Sussex for Arthur Annesley Voysey. AA Voysey was the architect's younger brother, a retired electrical engineer.

Brooke End, New Road, Henley-in-Arden, Warwickshire, for Miss F Wright.

Lodge Style, Combe Down, near Bath, for T Sturge Cotterell.

## 1911

House in Malone Road, Belfast, for Robert Hetherington.

## 1913

Pleasure Ground, East Row, Kensal Green, London, W10: a recreation park commissioned by EJ Horniman. Some 19 years earlier Voysey had designed Lowicks House for Horniman.

## 1919

War memorial at Malvern Wells, Hereford and Worcester.

Other designers contemporary with Voysey became involved in the design of war memorials. These included: Eric Gill, Detmar Blow, E Guy Dawber, HS Goodhart-Rendel, Selwyn Image, George Jack, WR Lethaby, Mervyn Macartney and Omar Ramsden, See Lawrence Weaver's book, *Memorials and Monuments*, London, 1915.

## 1920

War Memorial, Potter's Bar, Hertfordshire.

From 1920 until the mid-30s, Voysey designed fabrics, carpets, wallpapers, and very occasionally, furniture.

LODGE STYLE, 1909

# BIBLIOGRAPHY

**Writings by Voysey**

'Domestic Furniture', *Journal of the Royal Institute of British Architects*, I, 1894.

'Ideas in Things' in *The Arts Connected with Building*, (edited by T Raffles Davison), Batsford, London, 1909.

*Individuality*, Chapman & Hall, London, 1915.

Introduction to a catalogue of an exhibition of the work of CFA Voysey at the Batsford Gallery, 1931.

'The Aims and Conditions of the Modern Decorator', *The Journal of Decorative Art*, XV, 1895.

'"The Orchard", Chorleywood, Herts', *Architectural Review*, X, 1901.

A contribution to 'L'Art Nouveau: what it is and what is thought of it – a symposium', *Magazine of Art*, II, 1904.

'Patriotism in Architecture', *Journal of the Architectural Association*, XXVIII, 1912.

'The Quality of Fitness in Architecture', *The Craftsman*, XXIII, 1912.

*Tradition and Individuality in Art*, 1923. An unpublished typescript in the Library of the Royal Institute of British Architects.

*Reason as a Basis of Art*, Elkin Mathews, London, 1906.

*Symbolism in Design*, 1930. An unpublished manuscript in the Library of the Royal Institute of British Architects.

*The Value of Hidden Influences as Disclosed in the Life of One Ordinary Man*, 1931. An unpublished manuscript in the Library of the Royal Institute of British Architects.

Letter to the Editor, *Architects' Journal*, LXXXI, 1935.

Much of Voysey's correspondence survives in private hands. It has not been catalogued.

**Books on Voysey**

Adams, Maurice B, *Modern Cottage Architecture*, illustrated from works by well-known architects, London, 1904.

Allibone, Jill, *George Devey*, Cambridge, 1991.

*Arts and Crafts Essays by Members of the Arts and Crafts Exhibition Society*, with a Preface by William Morris, London, 1893.

Aslin, Elizabeth, *The Aesthetic Movement: Prelude to Art Nouveau*, London, 1969.

Banham, Reyner, *Theory and Design in the First Machine Age*, London, 1960, (new edition 1980).

Brandon-Jones, John, *CFA Voysey, a Memoir*, The Architectural Association, London, no date (1957).

Cassou, Langui and Pevsner, *The Sources of Modern Art*, London, 1962, (German edition, Munich, 1961).

Cloag, John, *The English Tradition in Design*, London, 1947.

Crook, J Mordaunt, *The Dilemma of Style: Architectural Ideas from the Picturesque to the Post-Modern*, London, 1987.

Davey, Peter, *Arts and Crafts Architecture: The Search for Earthly Paradise*, London, 1980.

Davison, T Raffles, *Modern Homes*, London, 1909.

Durant, Stuart, *The Decorative Designs of CFA Voysey: From the Drawings Collection of The British Architectural Library, The Royal Institute of British Architects*, Cambridge, 1990, (New York, 1991).

Elder-Duncan, JH, *Country Cottages and Week-End Homes*, London, 1906.

Faber, Geoffrey, *Oxford Apostles: A character study of the Oxford Movement*, London, 1933.

Farr, Dennis, *English Art, 1870-1940*, Oxford, 1978, (*Oxford History of English Art* series).

Ferriday, Peter, (editor) *Victorian Architecture*, with an Introduction by John Betjeman, London, 1968. See Brandon-Jones, John, 'CFA Voysey'.

Gebhard, David, *Charles FA Voysey, Architect*, Los Angeles, 1975.

Girouard, Mark, *Sweetness and Light: The Queen Anne Movement, 1860-1900*, Oxford, 1977; *The Victorian Country House*, Oxford, 1971.

Gradidge, Roderick, *Dream Houses: The Edwardian Ideal*, London, 1980.

Hitchcock, Henry-Russell, *Architecture: Nineteenth and Twentieth Centuries*, Harmondsworth, 1958.

Holme, Charles, (editor) *Modern British Domestic Architecture and Decoration*, London, 1901.

Howarth, Thomas, *Charles Rennie Mackintosh and the Modern Movement*, London, 1952.

Jackson, Frank, *Sir Raymond Unwin: Architect, Planner and Visionary*, London, 1985.

Kornwolf James, *MH Baillie Scott and the Arts and Crafts Movement*, Baltimore, 1972.

Lethaby, WR, *Philip Webb and his work*, London, 1935.

Macartney, Mervyn E, (editor) 'Recent English Domestic Architecture', *Architectural Review*, London, 1911.

McGrath, Raymond, *Twentieth Century Houses*, London, 1934.

Madsen, Tschudi, S, *Art Nouveau*, London, 1967.

Marriott, Charles, *Modern English Architecture*, London, 1924.

Mawson, Thomas H, *The Art and Craft of Garden Making . . .* London, 1900.

Morris, William, *News from Nowhere*, London, 1890.

Muthesius, Hermann, *Das Englische Haus*, this edition, Berlin, 1908-11; *Landhaus und Garten . . .*, Munich, 1910, (first edition 1907); *Das moderne Landhaus und seine innere Austaltung*, Munich, 1905.

Nairn, Ian and Pevsner, Nikolaus, *The Buildings of England: Surrey*, Harmondsworth, 1962.

Naylor, Gillian, *The Arts and Crafts Movement*, London, 1971.

Pevsner, Nikolaus, *Pioneers of the Modern Movement: From William Morris to Walter Gropius*, London, 1936, (first reprinted, with revisions, as *Pioneers of Modern Design*, New York, 1949); 'Studies in Art', *Architecture and Design, Volume 2, Victorian and After*, London, 1968; see 'CFA Voysey', which first appeared in *Elseviers Mandschrift*, May 1940, (translated by Caroline Doggart and revised by Nikolaus Pevsner). See also: 'A Mackmurdo', which first appeared in *Architectural Review*, LXXXIII, 1938.

Pugin, AWN, *Contrasts*, London, 1841, (first edition, 1836); *The True Principles of Pointed or Christian Architecture*, London, 1841.

Richards, JM, *An Introduction to Modern Architecture*, Harmondsworth, 1940.

Ruskin, John, *The Diaries of John Ruskin*, edited by Joan Evans and John Howard Whitehouse, Oxford, 1956-59; *The Seven Lamps of Architecture*, London, 1949; *The Stones of Venice*, London, 1352-53.

Schmutzler, Robert, *Art Nouveau*, London, 1964, (German edition, Stuttgart, 1962).

Scott, MH Baillie, *Houses and Gardens*, London, 1906.

Service, Alistair, (editor) *Edwardian Architecture*, London, 1977; *Edwardian Architecture and its Origins*, London, 1975.

Simpson, Duncan, *CFA Voysey: an Architect of Individuality*, with a Preface by Sir James Richards, London, 1979.

Sparrow, Walter Shaw, (editor) *The British Home of Today: a book of Modern Domestic Architecture and the Applied Arts*, London, no date (1904); *The Modern Home: a book of British domestic architecture for moderate incomes*, London, no date (1907).

Voysey, The Reverend Charles, *Theism, the Religion of Common Sense*, London, 1896.

Watkin, David, *The Rise of Architectural History*, London, 1980.

Weaver, Lawrence, (editor) *Small Country Houses of Today*, London, no date (1910).

Wilmott, Ernest, *English House Design: a Review . . . .*, London, 1910.

Wittkower, Rudolf, (editor) *Studies in Western Art: Problems of the Nineteenth and Twentieth Centuries*, Princeton, 1963. See Summerson, John, 'Some British Contemporaries of Frank Lloyd Wright'.

Wrightson, Priscilla, (editor) *The Small English House*, a catalogue of books, B Weinreb Architectural Books, London, 1977.

Yorke, FRS , *The Modern House in England*, London, 1937.

## Catalogues

*Architect-Designers: Pugin to Mackintosh*, The Fine Art Society, London, 1981.

*Arts and Crafts Exhibition Society: Catalogue of the First Exhibition*, London, 1888. (Voysey exhibited in this and in subsequent exhibitions of the Society.)

*Arts Décoratifs de Grande-Bretagne et d'Irlande*, London, 1914, (this large exhibition, which was held in Paris, encapsulated the achievements of the Arts and Crafts Movement).

*Birth of Modern Design*, catalogue of an Exhibition, curated by Michael Whiteway, at the Sezon Museum of Art, 1990, (text in Japanese).

Brandon-Jones, John, and others, *CFA Voysey: Architect and Designer*, *1857-1941*, Brighton, 1978.

*Exhibition of British Design for Surface Decoration*, London, 1915, (the exhibition was mounted by the Board of Trade).

Floud, Peter F, (editor) *Exhibition of Victorian and Edwardian Decorative Arts*, London, 1952, (see Section S - CFA Voysey).

Gebhard, David, *Charles FA Voysey*, Santa Barbara, California, 1970.

*Great British Architects*, with an Introduction by Sir John Summerson, London, 1981, (catalogue of an exhibition at the Architectural Association: the architects are – Chambers, Searles, Pugin, Charles Barry, Voysey and Rickards).

(Mackmurdo) *Catalogue of AH Mackmurdo and The Century Guild Collection*, London, 1967.

(Muthesius) Sharp, Dennis, (editor) *Hermann Muthesius, 1861-1927*, London, 1979, (catalogue of an exhibition at the Architectural Association).

Oman, Charles C and Hamilton, Jean, *Wallpaper: a History and Illustrated Catalogue of the Collection at the Victoria and Albert Museum*, London, 1983.

Parry, Linda, *Textiles of the Arts and Crafts Movement*, London, 1988.

Physick, John and Darby, Michael, *Marble Halls: Drawings and Models for Victorian Secular Buildings*, London, 1973.

*Les Sources du XXème Siècle: les Arts en Europe de 1884 à 1914*, Paris, 1960.

(Seddon) *Darby, Michael and John Pollard Seddon, Catalogue of Architectural Drawings in the Victoria and Albert Museum*, London, 1983.

Selz, Peter and Constantine, Mildred, *Art Nouveau: Art and Design at the Turn of the Century*, New York, 1959.

*Summary Catalogue of Textile Designs, 1840-1985, in the Victoria and Albert Museum*, London, 1988, (on microfiche – contains details of Voysey's decorative designs in the V & A's holdings).

Symonds, Joanna, *CFA Voysey: Catalogue of the Drawings, Collection of the Royal Institute of British Architects*, Farnborough, Hampshire, 1975, (indispensable in any study of Voysey – the RIBA hold the majority of his drawings).

## Selected Articles

An extensive list of Voysey's articles, published letters and manuscripts is contained in the Bibliography of Joanna Symonds' catalogue of Voysey's drawings at the RIBA – see under Catalogues. However, the following are listed for their particular interest:

## Writings on Voysey

Anon, (possibly Gleeson White), 'An interview with Mr Charles F Annesley Voysey, architect and designer', *The Studio*, I, 1893.

Anon, 'Art in Decoration and Design', *The Builder*, LXVIII, 1895.

Anon, (possibly Hermann Muthesius), 'CFA Voysey', *Dekorative Kunst*, I, Munich, 1897.

Anon, 'Houses for People with Hobbies: "The Orchard", Chorley Wood', *Country Life*, VI, 1899.

Anon, 'Houses for People with Hobbies: "Walnut Tree Farm", Castlemorton', *Country Life*, VI, 1899.

Anon, 'The Arts and Crafts Exhibition at the New Gallery', *The Studio*, XXVIII, 1903.

Anon, 'Some recent designs for Domestic Architecture', *The Studio*, XXXIV, 1905.

Anon, 'CFA Voysey, the man and his work', *Architect and Building News*, CXVII, 1927, (in five parts).

Anon, 'CFA Voysey', *Architect and Building News*, CLXI, 1940.

Anon, an obituary, *Architects' Journal*, XCIII, 1941.

Betjeman, John, 'CFA Voysey', *Architects' Journal*, XCIII, 1941.

Betjeman, John, 'CFA Voysey', *Architects' Journal*, XCI, 1940.

Betjeman, John, 'Charles Francis Annesley Voysey, the architect of individualism', *Architectural Review*, LXX, 1931.

Betjeman, John, 'CFA Voysey', *Architectural Forum*, LXII, New York, 1940.

Brandon-Jones, John, 'Architecture and the Art Workers' Guild', *The Journal of the Royal Society of Arts*, CXXI, 1973.

Brandon-Jones, John, 'An architect's letters to his client', *Architect and Building News*, CXCV, 1949.

Daryll, AB, 'The Architecture of Charles Francis Annesley Voysey', *Magazine of Fine Arts*, II, 1905.

Donat, Robert, 'Uncle Charles . . .'. *Architects' Journal*, XCIII, 1941, (a memoir, which was also broadcast, by the distinguished actor – who was related to Voysey by marriage).

EBS, 'Some recent designs by Mr CFA Voysey', *The Studio*, VII, 1896.

The Editor, 'Royal Gold Medallist', *RIBA Journal*, XLVII, 1940.

The Editor, 'The Royal Gold Medal Award to Mr CFA Voysey', *The Builder*, CLIX, 1940.

Fletcher, HM, 'The Work of CFA Voysey', *RIBA Journal*, XXXVIII, 1931, (a review of the exhibition at the Batsford Gallery).

Floud, Peter F, 'The Wallpaper Designs of CFA Voysey', *The Penrose Annual*, LII, 1958.

Frahne, HW, 'Recent English Domestic Architecture', *Architectural Record*, XXV, New York, 1909.

Furst, H, 'The Exhibition of the Work of CFA Voysey at the Batsford Gallery', *Apollo*, XIV, 1931.

'G', 'The Revival of English Domestic Architecture: the work of Mr. CFA Voysey', *The Studio*, XI, 1897.

Hellman, L, 'Voysey in Wonderland', *Building Design*, 169, 1975.

Klopfer, Paul, 'Voyseys Architektur-Idyllen', *Moderne Bauformen*, IX, Stuttgart, 1910.

Konody, PG, 'CFA Voyseys neuere Arbeiten', *Dekorative Kunst*, XIV, Munich, 1906.

Pevsner, Nikolaus, 'Charles F Annesley Voysey, 1857-1941', *The Architectural Review*, LXXXIX, 1941.

Richards, J M, an obituary, *The Architectural Review*, LXXXIX, 1941.

Richardson, Margaret, 'Wallpapers by CFA Voysey', *Journal of the Royal Institute of British Architects*, LXII, 1965.

Robertson, Howard, and Sheffield, Noel D, an obituary, *Journal of the Royal Institute of British Architects*, XLVIII, 1941.

Summerson, John, 'Mr Voysey: Veteran Gold Medallist', *The Listener*, XXIII, 1940.

Townsend, Horace, 'Notes on Country and Suburban Houses designed by CFA Voysey', *The Studio*, XVI, 1899.

Vallance, Aymer, 'British Decorative Art in 1899 and the Arts and Crafts Exhibition', *The Studio*, XVIII, 1899.

Vallance, Aymer, 'Some recent work by Mr CFA Voysey', *The Studio*, XXXI, 1904.

Van de Velde, Henry, 'Artistic Wallpapers', *Emulation*, XVIII, Brussels, 1893.

Van de Velde, Henry, 'Essex and Co's 'Westminster Wallpapers', *L'Art Moderne*, XIV, Brussels, 1894.

Verneuil, MP, 'Le Papier-Peinté à l'Exposition', *Art et Décoration*, VIII, Paris, 1900.

The Exhibition of Voysey's Decorative Designs at the Heinz Gallery of the Royal Institute of British Architects, in September, 1990. These inspired a number of short articles which have not been listed.

DESIGN FOR A FRETTED BRASS PANEL FOR A HOUSE IN HANS ROAD, KNIGHTSBRIDGE, 1891-92